DAMAGED

CHOICE CANDY
From Your Own Kitchen

**By the Food Editors
of Farm Journal**

Countryside Press
a division of Farm Journal, Inc.
Philadelphia, Pennsylvania

Cover and Book Design by Al J. Reagan

CHOICE CANDY
From Your Own Kitchen

Contents

How to Make Perfect Candy

How to Make Perfect Candy

Do exactly as your recipe directs when you're ready to cook candy. We list here some basic rules, but remember that there are variations to all rules. If the recipe you're using gives different directions, follow *your* recipe .

Use a fairly deep, large, thick or heavy saucepan with straight sides.

When you put the candy on to cook, stir it until the sugar dissolves and comes to a boil; then stir only enough to prevent sticking to the pan and scorching. Use a wooden spoon or your paddle-type candy thermometer.

Rinse and dry spoon before you use it to make cold water tests or to beat candy after cooking. This is a safeguard against grainy candy.

Cook candy at a fairly low, but steady boil. *Steady* is the important word.

When the candy mixture comes to a boil, remove any sugar crystals that form on the side of the saucepan. Do this throughout the cooking if necessary. To remove crystals, wrap a strip of cheesecloth or other clean cloth around the tines of a table fork. Dip in cold water, squeeze out the excess water and wipe off the crystals. Rinse crystals off the cloth and squeeze, so you'll be ready to wipe off other crystals if they form. Or dip a pastry brush in cold water and use it instead of the cloth-covered fork. Rinse sugar crystals off the brush after use, too.

Many candy cooks cover the saucepan for 3 minutes when the candy mixture comes to a boil. The steam dissolves crystals that form. Watch carefully that the syrup doesn't boil over. Put the candy thermometer into saucepan when you uncover candy. If crystals appear later, wipe them off with a damp cloth-covered fork or pastry brush.

When the candy is cooked (see tests below), remove the thermometer at once, or large sugar crystals may form around it and make the candy grainy. When the recipe directs you to cool the cooked candy, without stirring, to lukewarm, before you begin to beat it, be sure to cool it to lukewarm. Recipes often give the lukewarm temperature (110°), but don't worry about having removed the thermometer; it's easy to judge the temperature by feeling the bottom of the pan with your hand. It should feel neither warm nor cool. The candy will be grainy if not cooled enough; *sugar crystals form readily when you stir or beat warm candy*. It's better to have the candy mixture on the cool side rather than warmer than lukewarm. The cooler the candy, the more difficult it is to beat—but the creamier it will be .

Once you start the beating, keep at it until it is ready to pour or drop from a spoon. You need not beat it fast, but steadily. You can successfully use a combination of stirring and beating.

To pour candy into a pan to cool, bring the saucepan holding the hot mixture down close to the pan. Pour quickly and do not scrape out the remnants that stick to the saucepan. They may contain a few large sugar crystals—enough to spoil the entire batch. (Even one large crystal encourages other crystals to form and gather round. That's the way rock candy is made.)

Lightly butter, grease or oil pan before you pour the candy into it to cool. A heavy coating makes the candy greasy and less pleasant to eat from the hand.

If you aren't going to serve the candy shortly after it is set or firm, keep it in a cool place. In case you wish to keep is several weeks or longer, layer it between pieces of waxed paper in a container and cover tightly. Store in freezer.

HOW TO TELL WHEN CANDY IS COOKED

Cooking candy to the correct temperature is critical to success. There are two ways to find out when it is cooked enough—making the cold water test and reading the temperature with a good candy thermometer. FARM JOURNAL food editors make both tests and recommend that you do the same. You'll get a double check.

Cold Water Test: Remove saucepan of cooking candy from heat when thermometer in it registers at least 2° below the temperature specified in recipe. If you leave it on the heat until the temperature is reached, it can quickly overcook. Drop no more than ½ tsp. of hot syrup from spoon into very cold (but not ice) water. Let stand 1 minute. Pick it up with your fingers so you can feel the stage to which the candy has cooked.

Soft Ball: Hot syrup makes a soft ball when you pick it up, but it does not hold its shape (232 to 240°). For fudge, penuche and fondant.

Firm Ball: Hot syrup makes a firm ball that holds its shape when you pick it up (242 to 248°). For caramels and caramel corn.

Hard Ball: Syrup makes a hard ball. It feels hard when you pick it up, but is still plastic (250 to 268°). For divinity and taffy.

Soft Crack: Syrup forms hard, but not brittle threads rather than a ball (270 to 290°). For toffee and butterscotch.

Hard Crack: Syrup forms brittle threads that break between your fingers (300 to 310°). For brittles, lollypops and caramel or candy apples.

How to Use Your Candy Thermometer: Check the accuracy of your thermometer. Place it in a saucepan of vigorously boiling water for a few minutes. Then read the temperature without removing thermometer. It should be at 212° if your thermometer is accurate and you live at sea level. (Water boils at 212° at sea level, at lower temperatures in higher elevations. Subtract 1° for every 500 feet above sea level.) If water boils when thermometer registers 210°, it registers 2° low. This means your candy is done 2° lower than your recipe calls for. If water boils at 214° on your thermometer, add 2° to the temperature specified in recipe. Checking your thermometer enables you to correct differences due to the inaccuracy of your thermometer and/or altitude.

Many expert candy makers check their thermometers every time they make candy, for this also corrects variations due to weather. If you do not check your thermometer on rainy, humid days, cook the candy 1 or 2° higher than on less humid, fair days. Or cook it to a slightly firmer stage when tested in cold water.

You can put the thermometer in candy mixture before you start cooking it or when it comes to a boil. (If you cover saucepan when syrup reaches a boil and let mixture boil 3 minutes as a safeguard against sugar crystals forming, put the thermometer in when you remove the saucepan cover.)

Make sure that the boiling syrup completely covers the thermometer bulb and that the bulb does not rest on the bottom of the pan. A paddle-type candy thermometer with 2° graduations is an excellent investment.

Watch temperature closely after it reaches 220°. It rises fast after this point.

Read the thermometer at eye level. Hold it in hot candy in verticle position near the front of the saucepan. It is difficult to see the graduations, use a magnifying glass.

When the temperature reaches the temperature given in recipe, the candy is cooked. Remove thermometer at once or large sugar crystals may form around it and make the candy grainy.

Let the thermometer cool before you wash it, to avoid breakage.

Major Ingredients in Candy Making

Sugar is the heroine of the candy story. The way it behaves in the saucepan largely determines the quality of the candy. The first step is to use the kind of sugar specified in your recipe. Here are the types called for in this cookbook:

Granulated: This is fully refined sugar, in the form of small white grains. Take your pick of sugars made from sugar cane or sugar beets. You can use them interchangeably. When a recipe simply calls for "sugar" without a description, use this white sugar. Store it in tightly covered containers once you bring a supply to your kitchen. This will keep the moisture out. One pound measures 2¼ to 2½ cups.

Superfine: As its name indicates, this is an exceedingly fine granulated sugar. It dissolves so quickly it's sometimes called "instant" sugar. If your recipe calls for it and you do not have a supply in your cupboard, you can substitute regular granulated sugar. One pound of superfine sugar measures 2⅓ cups.

Confectioners': Many people west of the Mississippi River call it powdered sugar. It is granulated sugar that has been ground into a powder, soft and fluffy. It contains a tiny amount of cornstarch to prevent excessive lumping. Store it like granulated sugar in a tightly covered container. One pound, unsifted, measures 4 cups; sifted 1 pound measures 4½ to 5 cups.

Brown: All brown sugars, light and dark, are "soft" sugars, with a very small crystal size, which gives them their soft, spongy texture. The intensity of color and pleasing flavor comes from the amount of molasses syrup which clings to the crystals . . . the darker the sugar, the stronger the flavor. Store all brown sugars in airtight containers to retain the natural moisture. You can transfer sugar from package to wide-mouthed glass jars with tight lids and store in cupboard or refrigerator. Or you can pack it into plastic bags, close them tightly and put them in the refrigerator. Some brown sugar comes to markets in these bags. If brown sugar begins to get lumpy and hard, you can redeem it; spread it in a shallow pan and heat in a very low oven until it softens. Then use it promptly, for after cooling it gets harder than before. In this cookbook, unless otherwise stated, our recipes were tested with light brown sugar. One pound of light brown sugar, firmly packed, measures about 2⅓ cups; 1 pound of dark brown sugar, firmly packed, measures 2⅛ to 2¼ cups.

Colored Sugars: These sugar crystals come in a wide variety of attractive colors. You find them at your supermarket in tiny jars or see-through bags. Sprinkle them on candies for pleasing garnishes.

Cubes or Tablets: Because these sugars are a charming sweetening for hot tea, this cookbook gives directions for decorating them with tinted frostings in dainty designs. They add a pretty note to tea parties and, boxed with a frill of paper doily, they make delightful gifts.

Special Sugars: There are special sugars, but they are not available everywhere. Granulated brown sugar is one of these. It is free flowing. Frosting sugar, available mainly in the West, dissolves instantly and never requires sifting. The particles of confectioners' (powdered) sugar are processed so that they hold together in tiny balls, like popped corn in popcorn balls. It contains no cornstarch.

SYRUPS PLAY SUPPORTING ROLES

In the theater everyone tiptoes around the temperamental star, trying to humor her and save the show. If you think of sugar as the star in candy making, the syrups must be called the supporting players—they do such a lot to make the star look good! Give syrups credit for the marvelous creamy smoothness of fudge, divinity and penuche. Here's how sugar and syrup work together:

The big challenge every candy maker faces is how to keep the sugar crystals so small that no one notices them. Even the smoothest fudge or fondant, for instance, has tiny sugar crystals, but because they are small, you think the candy is creamy and smooth as satin.

It's natural for sugar, combined with a liquid like milk or water, to be grainy or sugary after cooking. Sugar is sucrose, which dries out and recrystalizes. Corn syrup, on the other hand, is largely what home economists call dextrose and levulose, or invert sugars. Instead of drying out, candies that contain sufficient amounts of invert sugars absorb moisture from the air and do not recrystallize. Also, during cooking, they invert some of the sucrose (granulated sugar). What corn syrup does is help prevent the formation of large sugar crystals.

Other food substances, such as lemon juice, cream of tartar and vinegar also keep candy from becoming sugary, but they're not so dependable as corn syrup. Grandmother had science on her side when she added vinegar to white taffy and made molasses taffy.

Here are some of the most widely distributed syrups for candies:

Cane: It comes in dark and light colors and is made from sugar cane.

Corn: Made from corn. this syrup can be either light or dark. The light syrup is bleached and clarified in processing; the dark is blended with refiners' syrup left after refining raw sugar. In our recipes we specify whether to use light or dark corn syrup. When you pour this syrup from the bottle, wipe the neck and recap the bottle tightly before putting it away in the cupboard. This makes the bottle easier to open the next time and helps prevent mold and crystallization.

Honey: The bees make honey from the nectar they gather from flowers; the flavor depends on the blossoms or fields they visit. There is more clover and alfalfa honey on the market than other kinds and jars are almost always labeled. Light color indicates a mild flavor. Strained honey, the kind used in candy making, is extracted from the honeycomb, strained and clarified. Keep honey tightly covered in a dry place. Chilling makes it cloudy. If it becomes sugary, set the open container of honey in a saucepan containing lukewarm water and heat until it becomes syrupy. The world's first candies and confections were sweetened with honey.

Maple: If your maple syrup is labeled 100 per cent, it is the boiled-down sap of maple trees. Since it takes so much sap to make a quart of this syrup, it is rather expensive. More widely available are maple sugar syrup (maple sugar with water added) and maple-blended syrup (a mixture of other syrups with some syrup made from maple sugar). Once you open the container of maple syrup of any kind, keep it covered in the refrigerator to discourage mold from forming. If mold appears, skim it off and heat the syrup to a boil, cool and refrigerate.

Molasses: This sweetener is processed from the concentrated juice of sugar cane. You can buy light or unsulphured molasses and a darker, sulphured molasses with stronger flavor, which results when sulphur fumes are used in the sugar refining process. Recipes in this cookbook specify when to use light or dark molasses. (Nutrition conscious candy makers never forget that molasses is a rich source of food iron.)

OTHER INGREDIENTS FOR CANDY MAKING

When Christmas is in the air, many women look in their cupboards and refrigerators to take stock of ingredients they'll need to make holiday candy. Here are some of the foods the candy recipes in this cookbook call for:

Butter or Margarine: Many candy cooks prefer the flavor of butter, but both margarine and butter contribute the desired richness. If you use margarine, either the regular or soft kind is satisfactory, although soft margarine contains less fat.

Cream: Recipes call for both heavy (whipping) and light cream. Whipping cream is available nationally, but in many localities light cream is not. You can substitute dairy half-and-half for it, but it contains less butter fat (10 to 12 per cent). Light cream has no less than 18 per cent butter fat. You can duplicate light cream by combining equal parts of heavy cream and 3 per cent whole milk. Dairy sour cream lends its delightful flavor to some candies and confections.

Canned Milk: Evaporated and sweetened condensed milk contribute frequently to the goodness and smoothness of candies. They are two entirely different products, and are not interchangeable. Be sure you use the one the recipe lists.

Dry Milk: This adds extra protein to some candies.

Flavorings and Extracts: While vanilla is the basic and favorite flavoring, there are many other exciting kinds that add variety in taste. It pays to buy well-known, quality brands. For economy, buy a large or medium bottle of vanilla extract instead of a small one. Keep the bottle tightly closed and as far away from oven heat as the size of your kitchen permits.

Some of the other flavorings called for in this cookbook are almond, lemon, orange, pistachio, black walnut, maple and peppermint extracts. Oil of peppermint, spearmint, wintergreen, lemon, orange and anise also are ingredients in some recipes. These flavorings, which you buy at drugstores, are so strong that you use only a few drops. When buying them, tell the druggist you will use the oil to flavor food.

Chocolate: Unsweetened chocolate squares, semisweet chips and squares, sweet cooking chocolate, milk chocolate and cocoa are all important in candy making.

Food Colors: The two types are liquid and paste colors. Both are certified by the Food and Drug Administration as safe. They come in a wide array of colors and you can mix them to make all the tints in between. You'll find liquid colors in practically all supermarkets. Some candy makers greatly prefer paste food colors, especially for hard candies; they contain no water. But either kind may be used with good results.

Coconut: Use the kind specified—the flaked shredded or finely grated cookie coconut.

Gelatin: Both unflavored and fruit flavored gelatins are important in candy making.

Fruits: Dried dates, apricots, raisins, prunes, figs and applesauce are the basis for excellent confections. Orange and lemon juice and grated peel also enhance the taste of candy.

Nuts: Adding different kinds of nuts to candies and confections is one of the enjoyable ways of providing flavor changes along with interesting texture. Among the kinds featured in our candy recipes are almonds, black walnuts, Brazil nuts, cashews, filberts, peanuts, pistachio nuts, pecans, walnuts and mixed nuts. Hickory nuts and butternuts are available in some country kitchens and many of the recipes sent by Oregon and California women call for walnuts. They explain that walnut trees grow near their ranch homes, often in their yards. Southern homemakers contribute recipes rich and luscious with their native pecans. Black walnut trees grow in a wide area and their fruit still holds the affection of many farm candy makers.

If you shell your nuts, keep the kernels in covered containers or tightly closed plastic bags. Put them in the freezer or refrigerator. If you buy shelled nuts in plastic bags, cans or glass jars, also keep them, after opening, in the freezer or refrigerator. Use unsalted nuts unless recipe specifies the salted kind.

Marshmallows and Marshmallow Creme: Both regular size and miniature marshmallows contribute smoothness and flavor to candies. Once you open the package rewrap them and keep them in the freezer. Marshmallow creme is an important ingredient in the newer type fudges.

Popcorn: Some time when you're in a supermarket, take stock of the many kinds of popcorn confections. You may be surprised how numerous they are. And look at the collection of recipes for similar snacks in this cookbook. Many women fix them in their country kitchens. Just reading the recipes will make you downright hungry and eager to start cooking some wonderful treats.

Equipment for Candy Making

Heavy Saucepans with straight sides in 2-qt., 3-qt. and 4-qt. or larger sizes. Deep saucepans are desirable because liquid evaporates too fast in shallow pans.

Double Boiler in 1½-qt., 2-qt. or 3-qt. sizes

Candy Thermometer of the paddle type with 2° graduations

Food chopper (Grinder)

Pastry Brush

Electric Mixer or Beater

Household Scales (optional)

Wooden Spoons with long handles

Broad Spatula with steel blade that does not bend easily

Pans for cooling candy: 13x9x2″, 8 and 9″ square, 15½x10½x1″ (jelly roll), 9x5x3″ and 8x4x2½″ (loaf pans) and baking sheets or large platters

Strainer

Grater

Kitchen Scissors

Wire Cake Racks

Knives for cutting candy and chopping nuts

Measuring Cups

Measuring Spoons

Bowls of various sizes

Wooden Skewers for lollypops and caramel or candy apples

Marble Slab or Plastic Kitchen Counter Top

Cast Iron (heavy) Skillet in 9 or 10″ sizes

Airtight Containers for storing candy

NOTE: Along with the equipment listed above, you will need waxed paper, and aluminum foil or plastic wrap.

CANDIES

Fudge

Memorable Traditional Fudge

When you hear someone speak longingly of "the wonderful fudge that Mamma used to make," you may be sure that Mamma had a good recipe—and a sure touch—for making classic fudge. This unforgettable fudge is the kind made with sugar, unsweetened chocolate, milk, butter, corn syrup, vanilla and nuts harvested on the farm.

It's difficult to imagine any more superior homemade candy than our Chocolate Fudge Velvet, Black Walnut/Chocolate Fudge or Blond Fudge Supreme. Our recipes for them are classics updated; if you're an inexperienced candy maker, follow these modernized directions, which eliminate guesswork, and you'll have good luck.

Avoid the two most common mistakes—beating the cooked candy *too soon* and *too little*. If you beat it before it cools to lukewarm, you can depend on grainy or sugary fudge. And if you stop beating it too soon, the candy will lack that marvelous creaminess for which fudge is famed. Beat it until a small amount dropped from a spoon holds its shape. Then pour it into the pan at once. If it balks on spreading evenly, just knead it gently a few times with your fingers until you can manipulate it. Even if it isn't satiny smooth on top, it will be creamy and delicious.

Chocolate Fudge Velvet

Creamy, luscious, smooth-as-velvet, classic fudge—sweet perfection

3 squares unsweetened chocolate, cut in pieces
1 c. milk
3 c. sugar
3 tblsp. light corn syrup
⅛ tsp. salt
3 tblsp. butter or margarine
1½ tsp. vanilla
½ c. chopped walnuts or pecans (optional)

Combine chocolate and milk in 3-qt. heavy saucepan. Cook over low heat, stirring constantly, until milk is scalded and chocolate is melted. Stir in sugar, corn syrup and salt.

Cook over medium heat, stirring until sugar dissolves. If sugar crystals form on sides of pan, wipe them off.

Cook without stirring until mixture reaches the soft ball stage (236 to 238°).

Remove from heat; add butter without stirring. Let stand without disturbing until mixture cools to lukewarm (110°).

Add vanilla. Beat until candy loses its gloss and starts to thicken. Stir in nuts and pour quickly into a lightly buttered 8″ square pan. (Do not scrape pan.) Mark in 36 pieces while still warm; when cold and firm, cut. Makes about 1½ pounds.

NOTE: You can substitute ½ c. cocoa for the chocolate. Add it to the sugar and salt (in saucepan) and mix thoroughly. Then add milk and corn syrup and cook as for Chocolate Fudge Velvet. Increase butter or margarine from 3 tblsp. to ⅓ c.

Kneaded Chocolate Fudge

Ideal candy for mailing—pack unsliced rolls in cans or mailing tubes

2   squares unsweetened chocolate,
       cut in pieces
1   c. milk
3   c. sugar
¼   c. light corn syrup
⅛   tsp. salt
1   tsp. vinegar
2   tblsp. butter or margarine
1   tsp. vanilla
½   c. chopped nuts

Combine chocolate and milk in 3-qt. heavy saucepan. Cook over low heat, stirring constantly, until milk is scalded and chocolate is melted. Stir in sugar, corn syrup and salt.

Place over medium heat and stir until sugar dissolves. If sugar crystals form on sides of pan, wipe them off. Cook at a steady, fairly low boil without stirring to the soft ball stage (238°). Remove from heat. Very gently stir in vinegar. Add butter without stirring. Cool until lukewarm (110°).

Add vanilla and beat until candy loses its gloss and starts to thicken. Stir in nuts.

Pour into lightly buttered pan or large platter. Let stand until cool enough to knead. Knead with fingers about 5 minutes.

Shape into 2 rolls, each about 2″ in diameter and about 5″ long. Wrap in waxed paper or foil and store in refrigerator or other cool place until ready to use. Slice slightly on diagonal in ½″ slices, wiping knife during cutting if fudge sticks to its blade. Makes 20 to 22 slices, or about 2 pounds.

Candy Christmas Trees: From an Iowa farm kitchen comes this suggestion: Knead fudge and mold in lightly oiled or buttered Christmas tree gelatin salad molds (3½″ long and 3″ wide in broadest part is a good size). Cool and unmold. With a little encouragement from a knife at the base, the "trees" slip out easily. Decorate simply with white or tinted Royal Icing (see Index).

Extra-Good Black Walnut Fudge

No reward for gathering, cracking and "picking out" black walnuts appeals more than a chance to help yourself to homemade candy in which the nuts star, according to a Kansas rancher on whose place several walnut trees grow along the creek. He rates Black Walnut/Chocolate Fudge one of the joys of country eating.

"Every year, as Christmas approaches," his daughter says, "Mother and I add our black walnuts to the fudge we make. This candy is our special gift to my aunts and uncles in Kansas City, who tell us the walnuts from the home ranch have an especially fresh taste lacking in nuts they buy in city shops. Maybe it's their imagination, but we all think the candy is exceptionally good."

Black Walnut/Chocolate Fudge

Black walnuts and chocolate go together like peaches and cream.

2   squares unsweetened chocolate,
       cut in pieces
¾   c. milk
1   tblsp. light corn syrup
2   c. sugar
⅛   tsp. salt
2   tblsp. butter or margarine
1   tsp. vanilla
1   c. coarsely choped black walnuts

Combine chocolate and milk in 2-qt. heavy saucepan. Cook over low heat, stirring constantly, until milk is scalded and chocolate is melted. Stir in corn syrup, sugar and salt.

Place over medium heat and stir until sugar is dissolved. If sugar crystals form on sides of pan, wipe them off. Cook without stirring at a fairly low boil to the soft ball stage (236°). Remove from heat. Add butter without stirring; cool to lukewarm (110°).

Add vanilla. Beat until candy loses its gloss and begins to thicken. Quickly stir in walnuts. Turn at once into a lightly buttered 8" square pan. While warm, mark in 18 pieces.

When cool and firm, cut. Makes 1½ pounds.

NOTE: If black walnuts are not available, use chopped walnuts and add a few drops black walnut extract along with the vanilla.

Peanut Butter Fudge

Peanut butter fans vote for this creamy chocolate candy

3   c. sugar
¼   tsp. salt
3   squares unsweetened chocolate
1   c. milk
2   tblsp. light corn syrup
1   tsp. vanilla
¼   c. peanut butter
1   c. coarsely broken nuts

Combine sugar, salt, chocolate, milk and corn syrup in 3-qt. heavy saucepan. Boil over medium heat, stirring until sugar dissolves. If sugar crystals form on sides of pan, wipe them off. Cook until mixture reaches soft ball stage (234°).

Remove from heat; do not stir. Let cool until the bottom of the pan feels lukewarm to touch (110°).

Add vanilla and peanut butter and beat steadily until candy begins to lose its shine. Add nuts and pour quickly into buttered 8" square pan. Cover and chill until firm. Cut into squares. Makes 36 squares or about 1½ pounds.

Slick Trick: Save the disposable foil pans which come with frozen and refrigerated foods from the supermarket. If you cool candy in these throwaway pans, you can cut it in neat, even pieces this way. Cut the corners of the pan, turn down the sides and slip the candy out in a block onto a cutting board. You won't have to dig into a pan to pry out the pieces.

Chocolate Chip/Peanut Fudge

If you like cookies with chocolate pieces, you'll like this candy

2   c. sugar
⅔   c. milk
1   tblsp. butter or margarine
1   tsp. vanilla
3   tblsp. peanut butter
½   (6 oz.) pkg. chocolate chips (½ c.)

Combine sugar and milk in 2-qt. heavy saucepan; bring to a boil, stirring constantly, until sugar is dissolved. If sugar crystals form on sides of pan, wipe them off. Continue boiling without stirring to the soft ball stage (236°). Remove from heat.

Add butter without stirring; cool to lukewarm (110°).

Add vanilla and peanut butter; beat until mixture begins to thickens and lose its gloss. Stir in chocolate pieces at once and turn into lightly buttered 8½x4½x2½″ loaf pan. While warm, mark in 21 pieces. Cool until firm, then cut. Makes about 1 pound.

Honeyed Fudge

Honey imparts that good, old-time country flavor to chocolate fudge

1   c. white sugar
1   c. brown sugar
½   c. evaporated milk or light cream
⅛   tsp. salt
1   square unsweetened chocolate, broken in pieces
⅛   tsp. baking soda
¼   c. honey
2   tblsp. butter or margarine
½   c. chopped nuts
½   c. cookie coconut

Combine white and brown sugars, evaporated milk, salt and chocolate in 2-qt. heavy saucepan. Cook slowly 5 minutes, stirring to dissolve sugars. If sugar crystals form on sides of pan, wipe them off. Add baking soda and honey. Continue cooking at a fairly low boil, stirring to prevent scorching, until mixture reaches the soft ball stage (238°). Remove from heat.

Add butter without stirring; cool to lukewarm (110°). Add nuts and coconut and beat vigorously until a little of candy dropped from spoon forms flat cakes. Pour into lightly buttered 8″ square pan; cool until firm. Cut in 36 pieces. Makes about 1½ pounds.

Distinctive Banana/Chocolate Fudge

If you salvage fully ripe bananas in your freezer to use later in banana bread, here's another sweet use for the fruit. It's a good idea to put the peeled bananas through a food mill, although you can mash them thoroughly, add a little ascorbic acid powder to prevent discoloration, put in airtight containers in measured amounts, label and freeze. Then the bananas are measured and ready to go. Of course you can make this moist, creamy Banana/Chocolate Fudge with fresh ripe bananas, thoroughly mashed.

Banana/Chocolate Fudge

Brown sugar, chocolate, vanilla and bananas mingle flavors

2	squares unsweetened chocolate, cut in pieces
½	c. brown sugar
1½	c. white sugar
1	medium ripe banana, mashed (⅓ c.)
¾	c. milk
⅛	tsp. salt
2	tblsp. light corn syrup
3	tblsp. butter or margarine
½	tsp. vanilla
½	c. chopped walnuts (optional)

Combine chocolate, brown and white sugars, banana, milk, salt and corn syrup. Cook over medium heat, stirring constantly, until sugars dissolve. If sugar crystals form on sides of pan, wipe them off. Continue cooking over medium heat, stirring occasionally to prevent candy from sticking, until mixture reaches the soft ball stage (236°).

Remove from heat. Add butter without stirring; cool to lukewarm (110°).

Add vanilla; beat until candy loses its gloss and starts to thicken. Pour into lightly buttered 8½x4½x2½″ loaf pan. Sprinkle top with nuts and gently press them into candy with spoon.

When cool and firm, cut in 32 pieces. Makes about 1¼ pounds.

Frosted Coffee Fudge

Unusual mocha-flavored sweetness — pretty to look at, good to eat

3	c. sugar
2	tblsp. instant coffee powder
⅛	tsp. salt
¾	c. milk
½	c. light cream
1	tblsp. light corn syrup
2	tblsp. butter or margarine
1	tsp. vanilla
1	(6 oz.) pkg. chocolate chips
¼	c. chopped walnuts

Combine sugar, coffee powder, salt, milk, cream and corn syrup in 3-qt. heavy saucepan (buttered). Bring mixture to boil over low heat, stirring constantly. If sugar crystals form on sides of pan, wipe them off. Cook, without stirring, over low heat to the soft ball stage (236°).

Remove from heat; add butter and vanilla; do not stir. Cool, without stirring, until lukewarm (110°).

Beat until candy begins to thicken; pour into buttered 8″ square pan.

Melt chocolate chips in top of double boiler over hot (not boiling) water. Spread evenly over cooled fudge; sprinkle with nuts; cut in 36 pieces.

NOTE: This fudge is not recommended for packing and shipping.

Blond Fudge Supreme

Serve this blond candy with dark chocolate fudge for color contrast

3	c. sugar
¾	c. milk
3	tblsp. light corn syrup
⅛	tsp. salt
3	tblsp. butter or margarine
2	tsp. vanilla
1	c. coarsely chopped nuts

Combine sugar, milk, corn syrup and salt in 3-qt. heavy saucepan. Cook over medium heat, stirring until sugar dissolves. If sugar crystals form on sides of pan, wipe them off. Cook at a fairly low boil to the soft ball stage (236°). Add butter without stirring; cool to lukewarm (110°).

Add vanilla and beat until candy loses its gloss and starts to thicken. Stir in nuts. Pour at once into a lightly buttered 8″ square pan. While warm, mark in 6 pieces. Cool until firm, then cut. Makes 2 pounds.

VARIATIONS

Coconut Blond Fudge: Substitute ¾ to 1 c. flaked coconut for the nuts.

Chocolate Fudge Supreme: Follow recipe for Blond Fudge Supreme, decreasing corn syrup to 2 tblsp. and vanilla to 1 tsp. Add 2 squares unsweetened chocolate, broken in pieces, to the sugar, milk, corn syrup and salt and cook, stirring constantly, until sugar dissolves. Then follow directions for Blond Fudge Supreme.

Superior Chocolate Fudge

This keeps well if you give it a chance—hide it in a cool place

4	c. sugar
1	(14½ oz.) can evaporated milk (1⅔ c.)
1	c. butter or margarine (2 sticks)
1	(12 oz.) pkg. chocolate chips
1	(7 oz.) jar marshmallow creme (about 2 c.)
1	tsp. vanilla
1	c. broken walnuts or pecans

Combine sugar, evaporated milk and butter in 3-qt. heavy saucepan. Cook over low heat, stirring frequently, to the soft ball stage (236°). It is important to stir frequently while cooking because mixture scorches easily.

Remove from heat; add chocolate chips, marshmallow creme, vanilla and nuts. Beat until chocolate melts and blends into mixture.

Pour into lightly buttered 9″ square pan. While warm, mark in 36 or 49 pieces with knife; when cool and firm, cut. Makes about 4 pounds.

Christmas Fudge

Delicious light brown candy dotted with red cherries and lots of nuts, including shaved Brazils—a big recipe for a Christmas special

3	c. sugar
1½	c. light cream
1	c. light corn syrup
1	tsp. salt
2	tsp. vanilla

1 c. diced candied pineapple
1 c. halved candied cherries
1½ c. shaved Brazil nuts
1½ c. broken walnuts
2 c. pecan halves

Combine sugar, cream, corn syrup and salt in 3-qt. heavy saucepan. Cook and stir over medium heat until sugar is dissolved. Cover saucepan and boil 1 minutes (this helps prevent sugar crystals from forming). Uncover and cook at steady, medium boil to the soft ball stage (236°).

Remove from heat. Add vanilla and immediately beat with electric mixer at medim speed. Beat until mixture is creamy and begins to hold its shape, about 10 minutes.

Thoroughly mix in pineapple, cherries, Brazil nuts, walnuts and pecans.

Press into 2 buttered 9″ square pans. Chill until firm enough to cut. Let stand in refrigerator 24 hours before serving. Makes about 128 pieces, or 4 pounds.

Best-Ever Chocolate Fudge

Milk chocolate gives this big patch of moist fudge its special taste

1 c. butter or margarine (2 sticks)
4½ c. sugar
1 (7 oz.) jar marshmallow creme
(about 2 c.)
1 (14½ oz.) can evaporated milk (1⅔ c.)
8 (1½ oz.) milk chocolate bars, broken in pieces

1 (12 oz.) pkg. chocolate chips
2 c. chopped walnuts

Combine butter, sugar, marshmallow creme and evaporated milk in 3-qt. heavy saucepan. Bring to a boil over medium to low heat, stirring constantly until sugar dissolves. Boil steadily over low heat 7 minutes, stirring occasionally. Keep mixture at a fairly low boil all the time. The saucepan will be almost full of the cooking mixture.

Remove from heat. Add milk chocolate bars, chocolate chips and nuts; stir until chocolate is melted and blended into mixture.

Pour at once into 2 lightly buttered 9″ square pans. While warm, mark candy in each pan in 64 pieces, or pieces the size you like; when cool and firm, cut. Makes about 5½ pounds.

Prize-Winning Fudge

Rich chocolate flavor is one reason this candy wins blue ribbons

1 (12 oz.) pkg. chocolate chips
3 (4 oz.) bars sweet cooking chocolate
1 (7 oz.) jar marshmallow creme
(about 2 c.)
4½ c. sugar
⅛ tsp. salt
2 tblsp. butter or margarine
1 (14½ oz.) can evaporated milk (1⅔ c.)
2 c. chopped walnuts

Put chocolate chips, cooking chocolate and marshmallow creme in bowl.

Combine sugar, salt, butter and evaporated milk in 3-qt. heavy saucepan. Bring to a boil, stirring until sugar dissolves. Boil steadily over medium heat 6 minutes (keep boiling all the time). Stir constantly to prevent scorching.

Pour boiling syrup over chocolate and marshmallow creme in bowl; beat until chocolate is melted. Stir in walnuts.

Pour into a lightly buttered 13x9x2″ pan. Let cool until firm. Cut in 77 or the desired number of pieces. When cold, pack in airtight containers and store in a cold place. Makes about 5 pounds.

Marshmallow Fudge

Very easy to make and good to eat—electric mixer does the work

½   c. butter or margarine (1 stick)
⅛   tsp. salt
1   (6 oz.) can evaporated milk (⅔ c.)
2¼   c. sugar
1   (8 oz.) pkg. marshmallows
1   (6 oz.) pkg. chocolate chips
1   square semisweet chocolate,
       cut in pieces
1   tsp. vanilla
½   c. chopped nuts

Combine butter, salt, evaporated milk and sugar in 2-qt. heavy saucepan. Stir and bring to a boil; then continue cooking at a steady low boil 8½ minutes, stirring constantly.

Meanwhile, combine marshmallows, chocolate chips, chocolate and vanilla. Pour hot candy over mixture and blend with electric mixer. Add nuts.

Pour into buttered 9″ square pan; cool. Cut in 1″ squares. Makes 81 pieces, or about 2½ pounds.

Confectioners Sugar Fudge

So tempting few people can resist it

2   (1 lb.) pkgs. confectioners sugar
2   (6 oz.) cans evaporated milk (1⅓ c.)
2   tblsp. butter
2   (6 oz.) pkgs. chocolate chips
6   tblsp. marshmallow creme
1   c. chopped nuts

Combine sugar, milk and butter in 3-qt. heavy saucepan. Bring to a boil, stirring constantly. Boil 4 minutes.

Add chocolate chips and marshmallow creme. Beat until chocolate melts and fudge thickens. Add nuts.

Turn into buttered 8″ square pan. When cool and firm, cut in 36 or 49 pieces. Makes about 3 pounds.

Quick Chocolate Fudge

It tastes like candy the experts make, and it's failure-proof

3   tblsp. butter or margarine
3   tblsp. water
1   (14 oz.) pkg. chocolate fudge
       frosting mix
½   c. chopped or broken walnuts or pecans

Put butter and water in top of double

boiler. Heat until butter melts. Blend in frosting mix until mixture is smooth.

Cook over rapidly boiling water 5 minutes, stirring occasionally. Stir in nuts. Pour into buttered 9x5x3″ loaf pan. Let cool until firm. Cut in 32 pieces. Makes about 1 pound.

VARIATIONS

Quick Nut Clusters: Omit chopped nuts from Quick Chocolate Fudge. Stir in 2 c. pecan or walnut halves or whole almonds. Instead of pouring into pan, drop from teaspoon onto waxed paper. Cool until firm. Makes about 40 clusters, or 1½ pounds.

Quick Marshmallow Fudge: Follow recipe for Quick Chocolate Fudge, but add 1 c. miniature marshmallows with the chopped nuts. Pour into loaf pan to cool, then cut in 32 pieces.

Double Boiler Chocolate Fudge

Candy with a different texture; a splendid stuffing for pitted dates

¼ c. butter or margarine (½ stick)
3 squares unsweetened chocolate,
      cut in pieces
1 lb. confectioners sugar
⅓ c. nonfat dry milk powder
½ c. light corn syrup
1 tblsp. water
1 tsp. vanilla
½ c. chopped nuts

Melt butter and chocolate in top of 2-qt. double boiler, or in saucepan over hot water.

Meanwhile, sift together confectioners sugar and dry milk powder; set aside.

Stir corn syrup, water and vanilla into chocolate mixture over hot water. Blend in sugar-dry milk mixture, half at a time, stirring until well blended and smooth.

Remove from boiling water. Stir in nuts. Turn into lightly buttered 8″ square pan. Cool, then cut in 36 pieces. Makes about 2 pounds.

VARIATIONS

Double Boiler Blond Fudge: Omit chocolate and water from Double Boiler Chocolate Fudge. Increase vanilla from 1 tsp. to 2 tsp.

Double Boiler Brown Sugar Fudge: Omit chocolate and water from Double Boiler Chocolate Fudge. Melt ½ c. brown sugar with butter and use dark rather than light corn syrup.

Double Boiler Peanut Fudge: Omit chocolate and water from Double Boiler Chocolate Fudge. Melt ⅓ c. smooth or crunchy peanut butter with the butter.

Double Boiler Marshmallow Fudge: Substitute 1 c. miniature or cut-up marshmallows for chopped nuts in Double Boiler Chocolate Fudge.

Date/Nut Fudge

For a change, shape candy in balls and roll in finely chopped nuts

4 c. sugar
1 (14½ oz.) can evaporated milk (1⅔ c.)
2 tblsp. light corn syrup
1 (8 oz.) pkg. pitted dates, cut up (1 c.)
2 tblsp. butter or margarine
2 tsp. vanilla
½ c. chopped walnuts

Combine sugar, evaporated milk and corn syrup in 3-qt. heavy saucepan. Cook over medium heat, stirring to dissolve sugar, until mixture reaches boiling point. Add dates and cook over low heat, stirring to prevent scorching, until mixture reaches the soft ball stage (236°). Remove from heat.

Add butter without stirring; cool to lukewarm (110°). Add vanilla and beat until mixture becomes creamy and thickens.

Pour at once into a lightly buttered 9″ square pan. Sprinkle with nuts, gently pressing them into candy. Mark in 49 pieces; when cool and firm, cut. Makes 2½ pounds.

Four Fudges from One Recipe

You can increase the appeal of any gift box or plate of homemade candy by including a few variations in the shape and/or color of the pieces. For white notes, White Almond and Coconut White Fudges fill the bill splendidly. And Cherry/Date White Fudge charms everyone who sees and tastes. Chocolate/Walnut Fudge, tempting balls rolled in chocolate shot, is irresistible. Fortunately, the electric mixer does the work in making these uncooked candies. The creamy richness comes from cream cheese. Even though the sweets are easy to make, the woman who fixes them gets generous bouquets from everyone who samples. The candies *taste that good!*

White Almond Fudge

Easy to make—no cooking, testing for doneness or beating by hand

1   (3 oz.) pkg. cream cheese
2½ c. sifted confectioners sugar
¼   to ½ tsp. almond extract
½   c. chopped almonds
⅛   tsp. salt

Beat cream cheese until smooth and soft with electric mixer set at cream (or beat with a spoon). Then slowly blend in remaining ingredients.

Press into a buttered 9x5x3″ loaf pan. Chill until firm, then cut in 21 pieces. Makes about 1 pound.

VARIATIONS

Chocolate/Walnut Fudge: Add 2 squares semisweet chocolate, melted, to cream cheese in White Almond Fudge. When creamed, slowly blend in 2 c. sifted confectioners sugar, ½ tsp. vanilla, ½ c. chopped walnuts and ⅛ tsp. salt. Shape 1 tsp. candy into ball and drop into small bowl containing ⅓ c. (2 oz.) chocolate shot (jimmies). Roll ball in chocolate shot and place on waxed paper or buttered foil. Repeat until all candy is shaped in balls. Makes 30 balls.

Cherry/Date White Fudge: Substitute ¼ c. cut-up dates (snip fine with scissors) and ¼ c. cut-up candied cherries for almonds in White Almond Fudge. Use ¼ tsp. almond extract or ½ tsp. vanilla. Makes 21 pieces.

Coconut White Fudge: Substitute ½ c. flaked or cookie coconut for almonds in White Almond Fudge. Makes 21 pieces.

Christmas Cherry Fudge

Festive bright pink candy—include a few pieces in holiday boxes

1   (3 oz.) pkg. cherry flavor gelatin
3½ c. sugar
¼   tsp. baking soda
1½ c. milk
¼   c. butter (½ stick)
½   c. chopped candied cherries
½   c. chopped walnuts

Combine gelatin, sugar, baking soda and milk in a 3-qt. heavy saucepan. Cook and stir over medium heat until sugar is dissolved. Continue cooking without stirring to the soft ball stage (236°).

Remove from heat; add butter. Pour into a large buttered platter; cool without stirring until mixture is lukewarm. Then beat until mixture loses its gloss.

Quickly stir in cherries and walnuts.

Turn at once into a buttered 8″ square pan. When firm, cut in 2x1″ (about) rectangles. Makes about 28 pieces, or 2¼ pounds.

Cream Cheese Fudge

Excellent fudge without cooking—it's rich, luscious and creamy

1   (3 oz.) pkg. cream cheese, softened
1   tblsp. milk
2   c. unsifted confectioners sugar
2   squares unsweetened chocolate, melted
½   tsp. vanilla
⅛   tsp. salt
1   c. chopped nuts

Combine cheese and milk; beat until smooth. Gradually beat in sugar; then blend in melted chocolate. Stir in vanilla, salt and nuts.

Press into a lightly buttered 8″ square pan. Mark 24 pieces. Chill until firm, then cut. Makes 1 pound.

Popular Cheddar Cheese Fudge

Cheese fudge proves the inaccuracy of the old saying that there is nothing new under the sun. When a state supervisor of the school lunch program made some of this candy for one of our food editors, she removed any question there might have been about why the sweet was so popular with youngsters.

One of the splendid features of the candy, loaded with Cheddar cheese and dry milk powder, flavored with butter, vanilla and cocoa, is that the electric mixer does almost all the work. You do not even cook the fudge. It's ideal for serving to a crowd of youngsters. But pass it to grownups, too, for they'll like its creaminess, sweet chocolate flavor and the way it serves as a snack to satisfy appetites.

Cheddar Cheese Fudge

Cheese flavor is subtle in this creamy, no-cook, protein-rich candy

2	c. shredded Cheddar cheese (½ lb.)
1	c. butter (2 sticks)
½	c. cocoa
1½	lbs. confectioners sugar
1½	c. nonfat dry milk powder (½ lb.)
½	tblsp. vanilla

Have all ingredients at room temperature; combine in large mixer bowl. Beat until creamy (it may be necessary to moisten mixture with ¼ c. whole milk).

Put in buttered 9″ square pan; chill. When firm, cut candy in 64 squares. Makes about 3½ pounds.

NOTE: Drained maraschino cherries, flaked coconut, miniature marshmallows or chopped nuts may be added.

Quick 'N Easy Fudge

Let the children make this fudge—it's cream-colored and velvety

3	tblsp. butter or margarine
3	tblsp. milk
1	(14 oz.) pkg. white frosting mix
32	pecan halves

Put butter and milk in top of double boiler. Heat over hot water until butter melts. Add the frosting mix and stir until mixture is smooth and blended. Then heat over rapidly boiling water 5 minutes, stirring occasionally.

Pour into buttered 9x5x3″ loaf pan and at once press pecan halves into top of candy. (Do this while candy is warm or nuts will not stay in place when candy is cut.)

Cool until candy is firm. Cut in 32 pieces so there is a pecan half on top of each. Makes about 1 pound.

VARIATIONS

Peppermint Patties: Follow recipe for Quick 'n Easy Fudge, but omit nuts. Add ½ tsp. peppermint extract and 3 to 4 drops red or green food color to the hot candy. Keep candy over hot water and drop from teaspoon onto waxed paper, making rounded, but flat patties. While still warm, press tines of table fork across tops of patties to make a "ribbed" design. Makes about 48 patties.

Lemon Patties: Follow recipe for Quick 'n Easy Fudge, substituting 1 (13 oz.) pkg. lemon creamy-type frosting mix for the white frosting mix. Make like Peppermint Patties, adding ½ tsp. lemon extract instead of the peppermint, and yellow food color instead of red or green. Makes 48 patties.

Quick Lemon Fudge: Follow recipe for Quick 'n Easy Fudge, but substitute 1 (13 oz.) pkg. lemon creamy-type frosting mix for the white frosting mix.

Elegant Italian Cream Fudge

This creamy candy containing crisp nuts is a second generation recipe. The Indiana homemaker who passes it on to you inherited it, and the memory of the marvelous candy, from her mother. Now she makes it in her own kitchen at Christmas time or whenever she wants a big batch of candy.

Be prepared to stand over it while cooking. The mixture is thick and it sticks to the pan unless your spoon keeps it moving. And when you beat the lukewarm candy, let your electric mixer do the work. "My mother always made sure there were at least two of us on hand to help with the beating," the Indiana homemaker remembers.

If you fear you cannot slice the candy neatly, dismiss your concern. A sharp knife cuts easily through the whole Brazil nuts, and you have crisp, white nuts in rich brown candy. You can substitute other nuts for those from South America, but the Brazil nuts make the fudge special.

Italian Cream Fudge

There may be more delicious candy but we've never encountered it

6 c. sugar
1 (14½ oz.) can evaporated milk (1⅔ c.)
1 (6 oz.) can evaporated milk (⅔ c.)
2 c. light corn syrup
⅛ tsp. salt
1 c. butter or margarine (2 sticks)
1 tblsp. vanilla
3 c. whole Brazil nuts (1 lb.)

Combine sugar, evaporated milk, corn syrup and salt in 4-qt. heavy saucepan. Cook over medium to low heat, stirring constantly, until mixture reaches the soft ball stage (238°).

Remove from heat and add butter without stirring. Cool to lukewarm (110°).

Add vanilla. Beat with electric mixer at low speed until candy thickens and is very creamy. Stir in nuts quickly. Pour into 2 buttered 8½ x 4½ x 2½″ loaf pans; cool until firm. Remove candy from pans and wrap each loaf in foil or plastic wrap. Store in cold place. When ready to use, cut in thin slices. Makes about 5½ pounds.

Divinity and Nougat

Two-Temperature Candy Cooking

Some expert candy makers prefer to divide the cooking of divinity into two parts. First, they cook the syrup to the firm ball stage (248°) and pour about half of it over the egg whites, beating constantly. They cook the remainder of the syrup to the soft crack stage (272°) and slowly pour it into the candy, beating constantly. A candy thermometer and the electric mixer are required for this method.

It's more work to make divinity this way, but some of our taste-testers think the candy is a trifle creamier and softer than divinity cooked to one temperature. You'll want to try our recipes for Double Divinity, either white or chocolate, and colorful Red Hot Divinity to find out which method you think makes the better candy.

Double Divinity

A 2-in-1 recipe—will make either chocolate or snowy white candy

2½ c. sugar
½ c. light corn syrup
½ c. water
¼ tsp. salt
2 egg whites
1 tsp. vanilla

Combine sugar, corn syrup, water and salt in 2-qt. heavy saucepan. Cook over medium heat, stirring constantly until mixture comes to a boil. If sugar crystals form on sides of pan, wipe them off. Reduce heat and cook without stirring until temperature reaches firm ball stage (248°).

Just before candy mixture reaches 248°, beat egg whites until stiff, but not dry. Slowly pour about half of the hot mixture over egg whites, beating constantly with electric mixer at medium speed.

Continue to cook remaining syrup to the soft crack stage (272°). Beating constantly, pour hot mixture, a tablespoon at a time, over egg white mixture, beating well after each addition. Continue beating until mixture begins to lose its gloss and a small amount dropped from a spoon holds soft peaks. If mixture becomes too stiff for mixer, beat with wooden spoon.

Mix in vanilla. Drop by teaspoonfuls onto waxed paper. Makes 27 drops or 1½ pounds.

NOTE: You can add 1 c. coarsely broken walnuts or pecans to Double Divinity. Mix them in with the vanilla.

Chocolate Divinity: If beating Double Divinity with electric mixer, add 2 squares unsweetened chocolate, melted, immediately after last addition of hot syrup; beat until mixture starts to lose its gloss. If beating by hand, beat 5 minutes after last addition of hot syrup to egg white mixture and then add 2 squares chocolate, melted, and beat until mixture holds its shape when dropped from a spoon.

Red Hot Divinity

If you enjoy the taste of cinnamon, you'll like this colorful candy

½ c. small red cinnamon candies (red hots)
½ c. hot water
½ c. light corn syrup
2 c. sugar
2 egg whites
1 tsp. vanilla

Combine cinnamon candies and water in 2-qt. heavy saucepan; cook until candies dissolve. Add corn syrup and sugar; cook, stirring constantly, until sugar dissolves. If sugar crystals form on sides of pan, wipe them off. Reduce heat and cook without stirring to the firm ball stage (248°).

Just before syrup reaches 248°, beat egg whites until stiff, but not dry. Gradually pour about half of the cooked syrup in a fine stream over egg whites, beating constantly with electric mixer on medium speed.

Continue to cook remaining syrup to the soft crack stage (272°). Add this syrup, a tablespoonful at a time, to egg white mixture, beating well after each addition with electric mixer or wooden spoon. Continue beating until candy starts to lose its gloss and drops from a spoon in soft peaks.

Stir in vanilla. Pour into lightly buttered 8" square pan. When cool and firm, cut in 36 pieces. Makes 1½ pounds.

VARIATION

Red Hot Coconut Divinity: Add 1 (3½ oz.) can flaked coconut with vanilla to Red Hot Divinity.

Sea Foam

Sea foams, half-sisters of divinity, are a bit harder, but luscious—Grandma liked the name and the candy

1¾ c. light brown sugar
¾ c. white sugar
½ c. hot water
¼ c. light corn syrup
¼ tsp. salt
2 egg whites
1 tsp. vanilla
½ c. broken walnuts (optional)

Combine sugars, water, corn syrup and salt in 2-qt. heavy saucepan. Cook, stirring constantly, until sugars dissolve and mixture reaches a boil. If sugar crystals form on sides of pan, wipe them off. Continue cooking, without stirring, at a fairly low boil to the hard ball stage (260°). Remove from heat.

At once beat egg whites until stiff. Pour hot syrup in thin stream over egg whites, beating constantly with electric mixer on high speed. Add vanilla; continue beating until candy forms soft peaks and starts to lose it gloss (this will take about 10 minutes).

Stir in nuts. Drop rounded teaspoonfuls onto waxed paper, swirling candy to make peaks. Makes 30 to 36 pieces, or about 1 pound.

Fruited Sea Foam

Mixed fruits sparkle in snowy candy

 3 c. sugar
⅔ c. water
½ c. light corn syrup
 2 egg whites
⅛ tsp. salt
½ tsp. vanilla
 1 c. candied mixed fruits

Combine sugar, water and syrup in a 2-qt. heavy saucepan. Cook, stirring constantly, until sugar dissolves and mixture reaches a boil. If sugar crystals form on sides of pan, wipe them off. Boil to the hard ball stage (252°).

Combine egg whites and salt, beat until stiff. Pour hot syrup over egg whites, beating constantly until mixture loses gloss.

Add vanilla and beat until mixture forms peaks. Fold in candied mixed fruit, reserving 2 tblsp. for topping. Pour into buttered 8″ square pan. Scatter reserved mixed fruit on top. When cool and firm, cut in squares. Makes about 36 pieces or 1½ pounds.

No-Cook Divinity

Pretty, airy and fast to make

 1 (6.5 oz.) pkg. fluffy white frosting mix
⅓ c. light corn syrup
 1 tsp. vanilla
½ c. boiling water
 1 lb. confectioners sugar
Food color (optional)
⅓ c. pecan halves (60)

Combine frosting mix, corn syrup, vanilla and boiling water in small size bowl of electric mixer; beat on high speed until stiff peaks form.

Transfer to large mixing bowl and beat on low speed, gradually adding confectioners sugar. Add food color if desired.

Drop by teaspoonfuls onto waxed paper. At once top each piece with a pecan half. Allow to dry 12 hours or overnight. Makes 60 pieces.

DELICIOUS ASSORTMENT—Chocolate Fudge, Seafoam, Divinity, Peanut Brittle, Christmas Ribbons, Nougat, Homemade Candy Bars, Anise Candy, Butterscotch, Lollipops and delicate Pastel Bonbons.

SPRING SELECTIONS—Unusual sweets in pastel colors fill a lace-lined box—perfect for Mother's Day or Easter gifts. Marshmallows, Open House Mints and Decorated Sugar Cubes.

HOLIDAY TREATS—"Stained Glass" hanging ornaments are hard candy poured free-form or into foil molds. On tray: Honeyed Popcorn, Apricot Nuggets, Peanut Butter Fudge and Holiday Logs.

EASY AND ELEGANT—Serve coffee and homemade sweets for an afternoon break. Napoleon Cremes, Anise Candy, little Bonbons (No-Cook Party Treats) and Old-Fashioned Butterscotch.

HOLIDAY PECAN LOGS—Delicious gift for any time of the year. Smooth, creamy, pastel-tinted fondant rolled in melted caramels and then in chopped pecans. It's easy to make, too!

LOLLIPOPS WITH FACES—Use your imagination when you make these whimsical pops. We decorated with lifesavers, but why not design your own creations using basic Lollipop recipe.

FACIAL TISSUE GIFT BOXES—Cut an opening on top of box. Glue cording to cut edge. Separate layers of candy with a cardboard. Cover with plastic wrap, taping to bottom of box.

Elegant American-Style Nougat

Nougat is the aristocratic, world-famous cousin of divinity. The Utah homemaker-home economist who contributed our recipe for the American-style candy says: "This nougat is so delicious that I have to hide it from myself after I've made it!"

It's truly delectable, even though the recipe eliminates some of the frills professional candy makers employ. For instance, classic nougat has very thin Japanese rice wafers on top and bottom. And it always contains honey, almonds (which have been blanched, shredded and toasted) and chopped pistachio nuts.

In our recipe corn syrup ably takes the honey role, and we omit the pistachio nuts. If you're making the candy for Christmas gift boxes or a holiday party, you may want to splurge a little by substituting 1 c. pistchio nuts for 1 c. of the almonds. Pistachios add a pretty touch of green and give an exotic flavor.

Even though American-Style Nougat is a simplified recipe, it still involves work—but is worth it. And you need to eliminate guess-work by using a candy thermometer. You can spread the work over two days if more convenient. Make Part 1 a day or several days ahead, cover it well with waxed paper and store in a cool place. It will be ready when it's time to pour Part 2.

Turn the block of firm candy onto a cutting board or surface and cut it with a sharp knife. The traditional shape of the pieces is rectangular and the size is about 1½" long, ½" wide and about ¾" thick. But we cut the candy in 1" squares. Wrap each piece in waxed paper immediately because the candy may become sticky if exposed to the air. Our recipe-testers cut 4½x4" rectangles of waxed paper for each piece and twisted the two ends.

Nougat has splendid keeping qualities when well wrapped and stored in the refrigerator or freezer. You can make it days ahead of Christmas for a holiday treat. Once you do, it's a candy you'll make every year when you start to think about Christmas trees and holly wreaths.

American-Style Nougat

The only thing more delicious than a piece of nougat is two pieces!

Part 1:
1½ c. sugar
1¼ c. light corn syrup
¼ c. water
3 small egg whites

Part 2:
3 c. sugar
3 c. light corn syrup
4 tsp. vanilla
½ c. melted butter
1 tsp. salt
3 c. blanched, delicately toasted and slivered almonds

To make Part 1, combine sugar, corn syrup and water in a 3-qt. heavy saucepan. Cook over medium heat, stirring until sugar dissolves. Continue to cook at a low boil to the soft ball stage on candy thermometer (238°).

When syrup reaches 230°, beat egg whites until they stand in peaks.

When syrup reaches 238°, add it in a fine stream to egg whites, beating constantly with electric mixer on medium speed, or with a wooden spoon, until mixture becomes thick and is lukewarm. It will keep several days if well covered with waxed paper and stored in the refrigerator.

To make Part 2, combine sugar and corn syrup in 4-qt. heavy saucepan. Cook over medium heat, stirring constantly, to the soft crack stage (275°).

Meanwhile, place Part 1 in lightly buttered large heavy bowl. Pour hot candy (Part 2) over it all ot one time. Mix with heavy wooden spoon. Slowly add vanilla and butter, continuing to mix with heavy wooden spoon.

Add salt and nuts, mix again. Turn into 2 well-buttered 9″ square pans, flattening top of candy with buttered hands. Let stand several hours.

Turn onto cutting board and cut each pan of candy into 81 squares, or the desired number of pieces, and wrap with waxed paper. Makes about 5 pounds.

Fondant

Fondant Delicacies

Fondant is a foundation candy. From it you build many tempting candies and confections that aren't identified as fondant. Chocolate creams with fondant centers are one luscious example. Mints in pretty, soft colors show up at supper parties and receptions—they're pure fondant. The candy also deliciously stuffs big, plump prunes and dates. And made into satiny coating, it covers almonds, raisins and many candy centers with beauty and marvelous flavor.

Some candy makers, failing to recognize what they can do with fondant, park their imaginations when working with it. Recipes for exciting fondant treats follow. Use them and the candy's popularity will skyrocket at your house. The first step, though, is to make fine-textured, creamy candy free from noticeable sugar crystals. Here's the way to do it:

Put candy mixture over low heat and cook, stirring constantly until sugar dissolves and mixture comes to a boil. Cover saucepan for 3 minutes while the candy continues boiling. Remove cover and cook without stirring at a steady, fairly low boil to the soft ball stage (238 to 240°).

Throughout cooking, keep sugar crystals wiped from sides of saucepan with damp, cloth-covered table fork or pastry brush.

Remove cooked candy from heat and pour at once, without scraping pan, onto a cooled, slightly damp baking sheet, platter or marble slab. A good way to cool the surface is to cover it with cracked ice. Wipe off ice and excess moisture just before pouring candy. Pour candy about ¼" thick.

Cool until lukewarm, judging temperature at center of candy mass with your hand.

Work with broad spatula or wooden paddle (you can buy these). Push the spatula under the edge of fondant and use a sweeping motion to the center and then back over to the edge. Turn candy frequently while working it. Work (beat) it until fondant turns white and becomes creamy.

Knead until smooth, giving special attention to any hard spots.

Add vanilla or other flavoring and food color if desired. Mix it in thoroughly. (If you wish, divide fondant in portions and flavor and tint parts separately. Then wrap and store in separate containers.) Or you can flavor and tint it when you're ready to use.

Wrap in waxed paper, put in a jar or bowl, cover tightly and store in refrigerator. Let mellow at least 48 hours or for several days or weeks. If fondant starts to dry out, cover with damp cloth.

Creamy Fondant

It's what you create with fondant that brings extravagant praises

2 c. sugar
⅓ c. light corn syrup
½ c. water
⅛ tsp. cream of tartar

Combine all ingredients in 2-qt. heavy saucepan. Cook over medium heat, stirring constantly until sugar dissolves and mixture comes to a boil. Cover saucepan for 3 minutes; remove cover and cook without stirring to the soft ball stage (240°). If sugar crystals form on sides of pan, wipe them off.

Remove from heat. Pour at once onto a cold, slightly wet platter or baking sheet. Cool until center of candy feels lukewarm.

Beat with spatula until white and creamy. Then knead with hands until smooth. Shape into a soft ball. Store in covered dish in refrigerator for at least 2 or 3 days before using. Makes 1 pound.

When ready to use, divide candy in 2 or 4 parts if you wish to make different kinds of candies or confectioners with the fondant.

Melt fondant over hot (175°), not boiling, water. Here are treats to make with it:

Autumn Candy Wafers: To ¼ Creamy Fondant, melted, add 2 drops yellow food color and 4 drops lemon extract. Stir gently just to blend. Drop from teaspoon onto waxed paper to make 18 round wafers.

Fondant-stuffed Dates: To ¼ Creamy Fondant, melted, add 1 drop red food color to make a luscious pink and 2 drops vanilla. Stir gently just to blend. Remove from heat. Cool slightly. Stuff into 24 moist, pitted dates. Roll dates in 1 tblsp. confectioners sugar.

Nut Creams: To ¼ Creamy Fondant, melted, add 1 drop green food color and 2 drops vanilla. Stir gently just to blend. Remove from heat. Cool until firm enough to handle. Form into small balls with hands. Balls should be ½″ in diameter. Press each ball between 2 pecan halves. Makes 30 to 31 candies.

Fondant Kisses: To ¼ Creamy Fondant, melted, add ¼ c. finely chopped nuts and a few drops of vanilla. Stir gently just to blend. Remove from heat and cool slightly. Drop from teaspoon onto waxed paper to form small mounds. Shape mounds with fingers to give them peaks. Serve as is, or dip lower half of kisses in melted dipping chocolate or confection coating. Or dip entire kiss in the chocolate coating. A good way to do this is to insert a toothpick through the peak of each kiss, dip candy in chocolate and then stand it, peak side down, with end of pick inserted in Styrofoam until chocolate is firm. Repeat with all candies. Cooling the kisses on the wooden picks gives them an attractive chocolate peak. When chocolate is firm, remove picks. Makes 20 to 21 kisses.

Fast-Cook Fondant

Confectioners sugar sweetens fondant, easy to make and shape

1   lb. confectioners sugar, sifted
⅓   c. butter or margarine
½   c. light corn syrup
1   tsp. vanilla

Combine half of confectioners sugar, butter and corn syrup in 3-qt. heavy saucepan. Cook over low heat, stirring constantly, until mixture comes to a full boil. Quickly stir in remaining confectioners sugar and vanilla. Remove from heat.

Stir only until mixture holds its shape. Pour into buttered 8 or 9" square pan. Cool just enough to handle.

Knead until smooth. (If fondant gets too hard to knead, work it with a spoon to soften and then knead.) If you want to make different candies, divide into 2 or 4 parts. Knead in food colors and flavorings as desired. Makes about 1½ pounds.

VARIATIONS

Fast-Cook Chocolate Fondant: Sift ¼ c. cocoa with 1 lb. confectioners sugar. Then proceed as for Fast-Cook Fondant. Delicious for Fondant-stuffed Prunes.

You can divide Fast-Cook Fondant in 4 equal parts and with one part make each of the following:

Fondant-stuffed Prunes: Stuff fondant into 30 pitted prunes (one 12 oz. pkg.). Tuck a walnut piece into each prune alongside the fondant. You will need about ¼ c. walnut pieces. Coat prunes completely with dipping chocolate or chocolate confection coating, if desired.

Mint Patties: Knead 1 drop green food color and 2 drops peppermint extract into one part Fast-Cook Fondant. Shape in 15 balls of equal size. Flatten with hands to make patties. Press top of candy mints with fork having 3 or 4 tines to make decorative top. Or knead 1 or 2 drops oil of cinnamon, peppermint or cloves and your choice of other food colors into fondant instead of peppermint extract and green food color.

Fondant Bonbons: Knead ¼ tsp. almond extract into one part Fast-Cook Fondant. Shape in 20 balls of equal size with walnuts in center. You will need 3 tblsp. walnut pieces. Roll balls in 1 tblsp. red or green colored sugar and then in 1 tblsp. multicolored candy sprinkles.

Miniature Fondant Eggs: Knead ¼ tsp. almond extract and 2 drops blue food color and 1 drop green food color into one part Fast-Cook Fondant to make it a robin's egg blue. (Leave some of fondant white for candy eggs if you wish.) Shape fondant with hands into 162 tiny eggs. Lay on waxed paper. Decorate eggs with brown food color made by combining 2 drops red, 1 drop blue and 1 drop yellow food color. Dip a small clean paint brush with fairly stiff bristles into brown food color; push bristles with your thumb over candy eggs to speckle them with brown. Serve 3 eggs in each Tiny Coconut Cookie (recipe follows).

Tiny Coconut Cookies

These two-bite confectioners hold tiny candy eggs of robin's egg blue

½ c. soft butter, or ¼ c. butter and
    ¼ c. shortening
¼ c. brown sugar, firmly packed
1 egg yolk
½ tsp. vanilla
1 c. sifted flour
¼ tsp. salt
1 egg white, slightly beaten
1¼ c. cookie coconut
Miniature Fondant Eggs (see preceding
    recipe)

Combine butter, sugar, egg yolk and vanilla in mixing bowl. Mix thoroughly.

Combine flour and salt and stir to mix. Add to first mixture. Blend well.

Roll dough, 1 tsp. at a time, into a ball and then dip in egg white. (Use 2 egg whites, if necessary.) Roll balls in coconut to coat.

Place 1″ apart on ungreased baking sheet. Press thumb gently into center of each ball to make indentation. (The cookies when baked will hold fondant eggs.)

Bake in preheated moderate oven (350°) 10 to 12 minutes. Remove from baking sheet. Cool on wire racks.

At serving time, place 3 Miniature Fondant Eggs in the indentation in each cookie. Or if you prefer, you can make the candy eggs a little larger and put only 1 egg in each cookie. Eggs may be made ahead and stored in airtight containers, set in a cool place. Makes 54 cookies.

NOTE: To secure the Fondant Eggs in place, you can fasten them to the cookies with dabs of Royal Icing (see Index).

Decorated Fondant Candies

Among the recipes in this cookbook are treasured favorites from women to whom candy making is a hobby. One of these contributors, a home economist-homemaker, the wife of a north central Iowa farmer, teaches a course in candy making every autumn at her local YWCA. Her pupils admire her decorated fondant specials and especially her festive fondant mints.

She uses molds to shape many of these candies. Some of them are rubber, others are flexible plastic. They come in sets, which she sometimes cuts apart with kitchen scissors to divide with other candy makers. Among her favorite molds are those shaped like bells, which she uses for the Yuletide season, wedding receptions and bridal showers; diplomas, for high school graduation festivities; booties, for baby showers; hearts, for Valentine functions, and rose shapes—the flower candies are pretty for parties for any occasion.

This Iowa woman recently made and decorated 200 fondant candies for a big community gathering. She says she can keep them in fine condition up to two weeks; she recommends arranging the candies in single layers in shallow cardboard boxes, and keeping them covered.

The ingredients for fondant candies are inexpensive; it costs about 15 to 20 cents to make 50 candies. The greater expense is the time you spend in making and decorating them. You do divide the work, though, because you make the fondant ahead. You can go a step further and shape and decorate the candies and put them in the freezer until needed. Let them thaw before uncovering.

When the shaped candies are set, you remove them from the molds and add decorative touches with Royal Icing. You can flavor and tint it with extracts and food colors, and put it through a decorating tube, using tiny tips.

Here is the fondant recipe this Iowa farm woman likes best, with directions for making her decorated candies. We include for good measure some of her most praised variations.

Decorated Fondant Candies

Festive candies brighten parties—no wonder they're hostess favorites

2   c. sugar
1   c. water
⅛   tsp. cream of tartar
½   tsp. vanilla, or ¼ tsp. peppermint or
        wintergreen extract
Food color, as desired
Glycerin
Royal Icing

Combine sugar, water and cream of tartar in 2-qt. heavy saucepan. Cook over medium heat, stirring constantly, until sugar is dissolved. When mixture comes to a boil, cover saucepan and let cook 3 minutes. Remove lid and cook candy mixture without stirring to the soft ball stage (236°). If sugar crystals form on sides of pan, wipe them off.

Remove from heat and pour onto platter cooled with cold water. Let stand without moving until center top of fondant does not stick when gently touched with finger and bottom of platter feels lukewarm. It takes about 25 minutes for it to cool. (If in a hurry, pour fondant into 2 water-cooled glass pie pans or platters instead of onto 1 platter. It will cool in about 15 minutes.)

Stir and work fondant with spatula until it becomes creamy and white. Knead smooth with hands. If you want to flavor parts of the fondant differently, divide in 3 parts. Add flavoring extract and food color to each as desired; then knead to distribute. (The amount of flavoring listed with ingredients is for the entire batch. If you divide the fondant, also divide the amount of flavoring you add to each part.)

Place each part in a small plastic bag, close tightly and store in the refrigerator at least 24 hours, or for several days. (Fondant keeps a long time at this stage, but if you want to store it several weeks instead of days, add the food color and flavoring when you are ready to shape the candies.)

When you are ready to shape the candies, place a plastic bag of fondant in top of double boiler and set it over the lower section containing water heated to 175°. (You don't have to stir fondant in a bag as it melts, nor worry about it crystallizing on sides of pan.)

Meanwhile, prepare molds by coating them with glycerin. They must be ready when the fondant is melted.

When fondant is melted, lift out plastic bag. Quickly snip a small opening in one corner. The bag will be hot to handle, so either drop bag of fondant into another plastic bag (also with corner clipped), or into a funnel made of waxed paper or plastic wrap, or into a pastry bag if you own one.

Squeeze melted fondant into molds. As soon as candy is cool and set, remove from molds. (If fondant gets too cool, return bag of it to double boiler over warm water to melt again.) If candies have rough or pointed bottoms, turn them over as soon as removed from molds to flatten bottoms and make a smooth surface.

Decorate cooled candies with Royal Icing put through decorating tube. For Christmas, mold bell-shaped candies from white fondant and decorate each with 2 green holly leaves of green-tinted Royal Icing (made with leaf tip) and tiny red icing dots for holly berries. Trim fondant patties with tinted or white icing flowers, or as you like for bridal showers and wedding receptions. Or decorate bell-shaped fondant with yellow (gold) ribbons, or with the bride's colors for wedding bells. Makes about 1 pound fondant.

Royal Icing: Beat 1 egg white and ¼ tsp. cream of tartar, adding about ½ package (½ lb.) confectioners sugar, sifted, a little at a time or until peaks with a break form, but do not curl. Add a few drops of vanilla or other flavoring and tint as desired. Keep covered with damp cloth or tight lid until used.

VARIATIONS

Candies without Melting Fondant: Shape fondant with hands into small balls. Dust with cornstarch if necessary to prevent sticking. Also dust mold with cornstarch. Press fondant into mold and pop out. (You can manage with one mold because the fondant

sets quickly.) Turn all hand-molded candies over to dry on other side.

Snowballs: Shape fondant around little nut pieces to make small balls. Dip in slightly beaten egg white and then roll in flaked coconut. (Or make Nut Balls by substituting finely chopped nuts for coconut.)

Forget-me-not Bonbons: Dip small ovals of fondant in melted fondant. When coating is set, make a simple flower of tinted icing on each piece with the decorating tube and a forget-me-not tip.

Pastel Bonbons: Shape fondant in small ovals and dip in melted pink or green confection coating. A few of these candies add charm to your gift box.

Coconut Kisses

No-cook potato candy goes glamorous when coated with chocolate

1	lb. confectioners sugar
3	tblsp. instant mashed potato granules
6	tblsp. boiling water
¼	tsp. salt
3	tblsp. nonfat dry milk powder
1	tblsp. butter
1½	tsp. almond extract
1	(4 oz.) can shredded coconut

Sift confectioners sugar into 2-qt. bowl and set aside.

Prepare mashed potatoes according to package directions, using water, salt and dry milk powder. Add butter and almond extract.

Make a well in confectioners sugar; add warm potato mixture. Gradually work sugar in; mixture will liquefy at first, then thicken. Continue working in sugar and beating until mixture is thick enough to hold its shape, adding a little more sugar, 1 tblsp. at a time, if necessary.

Mix in coconut. Drop by spoonfuls onto waxed paper. Makes about 3 dozen pieces, or 1½ pounds.

NOTE: Candy may be made into balls in palm of hand, then rolled at once in toasted coconut. Or cool the candy balls until set, then cover with chocolate confection coating or dipping chocolate.

Sweet Potato Candy

You'll enjoy this tasty sweet from Mexican candy kitchens

    1   medium unpeeled sweet potato
    ¼   tsp. salt
    2   lbs. confectioners sugar
    1   c. flaked coconut
    1½   c. finely cut or ground nuts
    ¾   c. finely cut or ground light raisins
    1   tsp. vanilla or rum extract

Boil, bake or steam potato until tender; peel and put through food mill or sieve to remove any fibrous bits (you should have 1 c.). Turn into a 2-qt. bowl; add salt. Gradually add 1 lb. sugar; mixture will liquefy at first, then thicken.

After the first pound of sugar is worked in, add half of each: coconut, nuts and raisins. Add remaining coconut, nuts and raisins alternately with remaining 1 lb. sugar. Add vanilla. Mix until well blended.

Turn mixture out onto a marble slab, baking sheet or other surface and knead (this also can be done in a bowl if it's big enough).

Line two 12″ lengths of aluminum foil with waxed paper; dust lightly with additional confectioners sugar or coconut. Divide candy in half. With lightly buttered palms, pick up candy and form into a ball, then into a short roll in the hands. Place on waxed paper and continue to roll, working from center to both ends, holding paper firm with one hand while the other continues rolling until candy is about 1″ in diameter. Roll up firmly in waxed paper and foil and chill several hours.

Repeat rolling with other half of candy. To serve, cut in slices. Makes about 48 pieces, or 3 pounds.

VARIATION

Chocolate Easter Eggs: Form Sweet Potato Candy in small egg shapes and dip in melted chocolate.

Homemade Candy Bars

Homemade Candy Bars— Quick, Easy and Delicious

Our brand new candy bars are for busy women who don't want to dip individual pieces of candy in chocolate, or who don't have time to do it. You'll be surprised how fast and easily you can turn out the appealing candy bars. You spread a coat of chocolate or butterscotch on waxed paper, cover it with one of our good fillings, and spread another coating on top. When firm you cut the candy into bars—the results are amazing and delicious.

These homemade candy bars travel successfully because they lie flat in a box. Their individual plastic wrap or aluminum foil wrappers keep the fillings fresh and protect the bars against jostling from rough handling in the mail. The bars do not break or crumble easily.

Since the idea of homemade candy bars is new, they'll attract attention and sell well at food bazaars.

They're a nice addition to the lunch box because they eat well out of hand. You can make almost a month's supply, 24 bars, at a time, if you cut them the size we suggest, about 2½x1". (You can, of course, cut the candy into smaller pieces, like fudge.)

We recommend that you do not make these candy bars in hot humid weather.

Chocolate Coating for Candy Bars

Smooth and glossy dress-up for candy

1 (6 oz.) pkg. chocolate chips (1 c.)
2 tblsp. vegetable shortening

Melt chocolate chips and shortening over hot water. Stir until smooth. Use as directed in the following candy bar recipes. Makes enough to coate 24 (2½x1") candy bars (an 8" square of candy).

Peanut Creme Bars

You can use salted mixed nuts instead of peanuts—chop large nuts

¼ c. butter
⅓ c. dairy half-and-half
⅓ c. sugar
1 tsp. vanilla
3 c. confectioners sugar
1½ c. salted Spanish peanuts
Chocolate Coating for Candy Bars

Combine butter, dairy half-and-half and sugar in 1½-qt. heavy saucepan. Bring to a boil, stirring constantly. Boil 3 minutes.

Stir in vanilla, confectioners sugar and peanuts. Cool to lukewarm.

Spread half of Chocolate Coating for Candy Bars on waxed paper to make an 8" square. (Place an 8" square pan on waxed paper and mark around it with a pencil to determine size.) Slide waxed paper with chocolate onto a baking sheet and place in refrigerator a few minutes, or until chocolate is firm. Remove.

Spoon filling several places over the coating. Then carefully spread it evenly to cover coating. With a metal spatula, smooth top and sides of filling. (If filling is too thick to spread on chocolate coating, add enough half-and-half, about 1 tblsp., to make spreading consistency.)

Spread remaining half of coating over filling to cover.

Set aside until candy is firm and until it separates easily from waxed paper. (To hasten setting, place in refrigerator.)

Cut in 2½ x1″ bars, or in any size desired. Wrap individually in plastic wrap or aluminum foil. Makes 24 bars.

Almond Bark Bars

Wonderful flavors—creamy almond bark candy and chocolate

1   lb. white confection coating
¼   c. dairy half-and-half
½   c. sliced or chopped unblanched almonds
¼   tsp. almond extract
Chocolate Coating for Candy Bars

Combine confection coating and half-and-half; stir over hot water until coating melts. Stir in almonds and almond extract. Cool to lukewarm.

Spread half of Chocolate Coating for Candy Bars on waxed paper to make an 8″ square. (Place an 8″ square pan on the waxed paper and mark around it with a pencil to determine size.) Slide waxed paper with chocolate onto a baking sheet and place in refrigerator a few minutes, or until chocolate is firm. Remove.

Spoon filling several places over the coating. Then carefully spread it evenly to cover

coating. With a metal spatula, smooth top and sides of filling.

Spread remaining half of coating over filling to cover.

Set aside until candy is firm and until it separates easily from waxed paper. (To hasten setting, place in refrigerator.)

Cut in 2½ x1″ bars, or in any size desired. Wrap individually in plastic wrap or aluminum foil. Makes 24 bars.

Date Crispie Bars

Luscious crunchy filling attracts loyal supporters for these bars

½   c. butter
½   c. sugar
1¼   c. halved dates (8 oz.)
1½   c. oven-toasted rice cereal
½   c. broken or chopped nuts
Chocolate Coating for Candy Bars

Combine butter, sugar and dates in 2-qt. heavy saucepan. Cook over medium heat, stirring constantly, until mixture thickens. Remove from heat and stir in cereal and nuts. Cool to lukewarm.

Spread half of Chocolate Coating for Candy Bars on waxed paper to make an 8″ square. (Place an 8″ square pan on the waxed paper and mark around it with a pencil to determine size.) Slide waxed paper with chocolate onto a baking sheet and place in refrigerator a few minutes, or until chocolate is firm. Remove.

Spoon filling several places over the coating. Then carefully spread it evenly to cover coating. With a metal spatula, smooth top and sides of filling.

Spread remaining half of coating over filling to cover.

Set aside until candy is firm and until it separates easily from waxed paper. (To hasten setting, place in refrigerator.)

Cut in 2½ x 1″ bars, or in any size desired. Wrap individually in plastic wrap or aluminum foil. Makes 24 bars.

Date Confection Bars

The filling for these bars is thin but rich with a caramel-like taste

¼ c. butter (½ stick)
1 c. brown sugar
1 egg
1 c. halved dates
¾ c. chopped nuts
Chocolate Coating for Candy Bars

Combine butter, sugar, egg and dates in 1-qt. heavy saucepan. Bring to a boil over medium heat, stirring constantly. Boil 5 minutes. Cool almost completely, then stir in nuts.

Spread half of Chocolate Coating for Candy Bars on waxed paper to make an 8″ square. (Place an 8″ square pan on the waxed paper and mark around it with a pencil to determine size.) Slide waxed paper with chocolate onto a baking sheet and place in refrigerator a few minutes, or until chocolate is firm. Remove.

Spoon filling several places over the coating. Then carefully spread it evenly to cover coating. With a metal spatula, smooth top and sides of filling.

Spread remaining half of coating over filling to cover.

Set aside until candy is firm, and until it separates easily from waxed paper. (To hasten setting, place in refrigerator.)

Cut in 2½ x 1″ bars, or in any size desired. Wrap individually in plastic wrap or aluminum foil. Makes 24 bars.

Macaroon Fruit Bars

Chocolate coating enhances bright color of filling and adds flavor

1 (15 oz.) can sweetened condensed milk (1⅓ c.)
1 (3 oz.) pkg. strawberry flavor gelatin
1 (14 oz.) pkg. flaked coconut (4⅔ c.)
½ tsp. almond extract
Chocolate Coating for Candy Bars

Combine sweetened condensed milk (not evaporated) and gelatin. Stir in coconut and almond extract.

Spread half of Chocolate Coating for Candy Bars on waxed paper to make an 8″ square. (Place an 8″ square pan on waxed paper and mark around it with a pencil to determine size.) Slide waxed paper with chocolate onto baking sheet and place in refrigerator a few minutes, or until chocolate is firm. Remove.

Spoon filling several places over the coating. Then carefully spread it evenly to cover coating. With a metal spatula, smooth top and sides of filling.

Spread remaining half of coating over filling to cover.

Set aside until candy is firm (candy bars made with this no-cook filling take longer to set than many other bars) and until it separates easily from waxed paper. (To hasten setting, place in refrigerator.)

Cut in 2½ x 1″ bars, or in any size desired. Wrap individually in plastic wrap or aluminum foil. Makes 24 bars.

NOTE: You can substitute cherry, raspberry, lime or other flavor gelatins for the strawberry, and cookie coconut for the flaked.

Caramel Nut Bars

Top choice of several taste-testers

1 (14 or 16 oz.) pkg. caramels
¼ c. butter (½ stick)
¼ c. dairy half-and-half
2 c. confectioners sugar
¾ c. chopped walnuts
Chocolate Coating for Candy Bars

Melt caramels (light or dark—some packages contain both kinds) and butter with dairy half-and-half in 2-qt. heavy saucepan over low heat. Stir occasionally. When completely melted, stir in confectioners sugar.

Remove from heat and add nuts. Cool to lukewarm before spreading.

Spread half of Chocolate Coating for Candy Bars on waxed paper to make an 8″ square. (Place an 8″ square pan on the waxed paper and mark around it with a pencil to determine size.) Slide waxed paper with chocolate onto a baking sheet and place in refrigerator a few minutes, or until chocolate is firm. Remove.

Spoon filling several places over the coating. Then carefully spread it evenly to cover coating. With a metal spatula, smooth top and sides of filling.

Spread remaining half of coating over filling to cover.

Set aside until candy is firm and until it separates easily from waxed paper. (To hasten setting, place in refrigerator.)

Cut in 2½ x 1″ bars, or in any size desired. Wrap individually in plastic wrap or aluminum foil. Makes 24 bars.

Crisp Nut Brittle

With Classic Peanut Brittle you caramelize the sugar for a superlative, true caramel flavor. The other two recipes include light corn syrup as an ingredient, which helps to prevent candy from becoming sugary. You can use either the larger Virginia or the smaller Spanish peanuts, but if you choose the larger kind, remove the red skins.

While some candy makers try to cut peanut brittle, it's often impossible to do it. The classic way is to break it into irregular pieces.

To Blanch Peanuts: Cover peanuts with boiling water and let stand 3 minutes. Drain, run cold water over them and remove skins. Dry thoroughly before using.

Virginia Peanut Brittle

You make this paper-thin, light-colored brittle with raw nuts—a favorite of peanut growers' wives

2 c. sugar
1 c. light corn syrup
1 c. water
2 c. unroasted peanuts, cut in pieces
¼ tsp. salt
1 tsp. butter or margarine
¼ tsp. baking soda

Combine sugar, corn syrup and water in a 12″ heavy skillet. Cook slowly over medium heat, stirring constantly until sugar is dissolved. Continue cooking until mixture reaches the soft ball stage (236°).

Add peanuts and salt; cook to just beyond the soft crack stage (290 to 300°). Add butter and soda, stirring to blend (mixture will foam).

Pour onto 2 large buttered baking sheets or 2 inverted buttered large pans. Lift candy around edges with spatula and run spatula under candy to cool it partially and keep it from sticking. While candy is still warm, but firm, turn it over and pull edges to make the brittle thinner in the center. When cold, break into pieces with knife handle. Makes about 2¼ pounds.

Classic Peanut Brittle

Old-fashioned way to make up-to-date brittle super delicious

 1   tblsp. butter or margarine
1¼ c. salted peanuts, broken or cut in
       pieces
 ¼   tsp. salt
2⅓ c. sugar

Melt butter in small saucepan over very low heat. Add peanuts and salt. Let warm.

Put sugar in 12″ heavy skillet over medium heat. Stir constantly until sugar melts into a light golden brown syrup (use care not to scorch). Quickly stir warmed peanut mixture into syrup.

Pour onto lightly buttered large surface at once (a large baking sheet makes a satisfactory surface, as does an inverted large pan). Spread out with spatula.

With a big spoon and fingers, pull candy into a thin sheet.

Cool; then break in pieces with a knife handle. Makes 1¼ pounds.

Salted Peanut Brittle De Luxe

You need a candy thermometer for this recipe from an Iowa farm woman

 2   c. sugar
 1   c. light corn syrup
 ¼   c. water
1½ c. salted peanuts
 3   tblsp. butter or margarine
 1   tsp. vanilla
 2   tsp. baking soda

Combine sugar, corn syrup and water in a 3-qt. heavy saucepan; mix well. Cook over medium heat, stirring constantly, until sugar dissolves. Continue cooking, stirring frequently to prevent scorching, until mixture reaches 285°. Remove from heat at once.

Stir in peanuts and butter, and cook, stirring constantly with thermometer, until mixture reaches 295°. Remove from heat at once.

Add vanilla and baking soda, stir to blend (work fast). Mixture will foam.

Pour onto well-buttered marble slab or 2 large buttered baking sheets. Spread out as thin as possible with spatula. As soon as brittle is cool enough so that you can work with it (about 5 minutes), turn it over and pull to stretch as thin as possible. When cold, break in pieces. Makes about 2 pounds.

Butterscotch and Toffee

Butterscotch and Toffee

Butterscotch is really a brittle—but with one difference. It always contains a goodly amount of butter. That's the secret of why it tastes so marvelous.

Toffee is in this great candy family, too. It's less brittle and somewhat thicker than its relatives—and plenty good. Pour it out as directed, to cool until firm—then break it into irregular pieces. Or, if you prefer neat squares or rectangles of toffee, mark the warm candy deeply with a knife. Then, when it is cool, you can break it along the marked lines in evenly shaped pieces. Some candy makers pour hot toffee onto lightly buttered baking sheets instead of into pans. However, if you want to mark the candy into evenly shaped pieces, you'll find that the sides of the pan help keep the edges straight.

Old-Fashioned Butterscotch

Butter-smooth with a crunch

2   c. sugar
¼   c. light corn syrup
½   c. butter (1 stick)
2   tblsp. water
2   tblsp. vinegar

Combine all ingredients in 2-qt. heavy saucepan. Stir and cook over medium heat until sugar is dissolved, then reduce heat and cook at a medium boil, stirring as needed to control foaming and to avoid sticking as mixture thickens. If sugar crystals form on sides of pan, wipe them off. Cook to a hard crack stage (300°).

Remove from heat and let stand 1 minute.

Meanwhile, butter 2 sheets of aluminum foil and place on 2 baking sheets. Quickly drop teaspoonfuls of butterscotch onto foil, making patties about 1″ in diameter. Space them ½″ apart. If candy thickens so that it will not drop easily, set pan in hot water until it again is workable. Makes about 6 dozen patties or 1¼ pounds.

NOTE: Instead of dropping butterscotch onto buttered foil, pour it into a well-buttered 8″ square pan. When partly cool, mark in squares with a knife; turn out onto buttered foil while still warm and slightly pliable. (A knife or spatula inserted along one side will help release it.) When butterscotch has hardened, tap it with a mallet or wooden spoon to break candy into pieces along the lines.

Brown Sugar Butterscotch: Substitute 2 c. brown sugar, firmly packed, for the white sugar and ¼ c. molasses for the corn syrup in Old-Fashioned Butterscotch. Cook and handle as directed in recipe.

Perfect Butterscotch Patties: Instead of dropping butterscotch onto oiled or buttered foil or pan, spoon it into lightly oiled or buttered tiny muffin-pan cups (1¼″ in diameter). Make thin patties. Remove when cold. This tip comes from a creative Iowa farmer's wife, who makes wonderful candies and takes pictures of some of the beauties before her family and friends enjoy eating them. She adds a little yellow food color to give the patties a more interesting appearance.

Butter Crunch Toffee

Flavor and crunchy texture make this candy a winner every time

- 1 c. butter or margarine (2 sticks)
- 1 c. sugar
- 2 tblsp. water
- 1 tblsp. light corn syrup
- ¾ c. broken nuts
- 4 squares semisweet chocolate, melted
- ¼ c. finely chopped nuts

In 2-qt. heavy saucepan melt butter over low heat. Remove from heat and add sugar; stir until well blended. Return to low heat and stir rapidly until mixture reaches a full rolling boil. Add water and corn syrup; mix well.

Stir and cook over low heat to the soft crack stage (290°).

Remove from heat and add ¾ c. nuts at once. Pour into lightly buttered 13x9x2″ pan and quickly spread with spatula.

When cool, remove from pan and place on waxed paper; spread top with melted chocolate. Sprinkle with the finely chopped nuts. When chocolate is set, break in serving-size pieces. Makes 1¼ pounds.

Raisin/Nut Toffee

Raisins are the happy surprise in this candy from California

- 1 c. sugar
- ½ c. water
- ¾ c. butter (1½ sticks)
- 1 tsp. vanilla
- 1 c. seedless raisins
- 8 squares semisweet chocolate (8 oz. pkg.)
- 1 c. finely chopped walnuts

Combine sugar and water in 2-qt. heavy saucepan; cook over medium heat, stirring until syrup comes to a boil and sugar is dissolved. Slowly add butter and cook to the hard crack stage (300°). Remove from heat; add vanilla and raisins.

Pour into a buttered 13x9x2″ pan. When cold, remove from pan and place on waxed paper.

Meanwhile, melt chocolate over low heat, stirring constantly. Spread half of it on one side of candy; sprinkle with half of the nuts. Chill. Then turn toffee over and spread other side with remaining chocolate and sprinkle with remaining nuts. Cut or break in pieces. This candy improves on standing in airtight container with waxed paper between layers. Store in refrigerator. Makes about 1¾ pounds.

Double Almond Crunch

Toffee is chocolate-nut coated on both sides —it also contains nuts

    1   c. coarsely chopped almonds
    1   c. finely chopped almonds
    1   c. butter (2 sticks)
    1⅓ c. sugar
    1   tblsp. light corn syrup
    3   tblsp. water
    3   (4½ oz.) bars milk chocolate, melted

Spread almonds in separate shallow pans. Place in slow oven (300°) until nuts are delicately browned or until time to add them to candy. Watch carefully.

Meanwhile, melt butter over low heat in 2-qt. heavy saucepan; add sugar, corn syrup and water. Cook, stirring occasionally, to the hard crack stage (300°). Watch carefully after candy reaches 280°.

Quickly stir in warmed, toasted coarsely chopped almonds. Spread in ungreased 13x9x2″ pan. Cool thoroughly.

Turn onto waxed paper; spread top with half of chocolate and sprinkle with half of finely chopped almonds. Cover with waxed paper and turn over. Spread candy with remaining chocolate and sprinkle with remaining almonds. Set in cold place until chocolate is firm. Break in pieces. Makes 2½ pounds.

Almond Toffee

Try this almond candy—it's superb

    1   c. butter (½ lb. or 2 sticks)
    ¾   to 1 c. coarsely chopped blanched
        almonds
    1¼ c. sugar
    1   (6 oz.) pkg. chocolate chips

Melt butter over low heat in 3-qt. heavy saucepan, then add nuts and sugar. Turn heat to high and stir rapidly until color changes to a light caramel, about 5 minutes. Almonds will start to pop at this stage and mixture will have a compact appearance, yet be fluid enough to pour out. Do not overcook!

Remove from heat and pour at once into a slightly warm ungreased 13x9x2″ pan. Spread out as thinly and evenly as possible, to about a ⅜″ thickness (candy may not fill pan completely).

Distribute chocolate chips over hot candy and spread evenly when they have melted.

When cool, turn pan upside down on waxed paper; tap to release toffee. Break in bite-size pieces with a small household hammer. Or, turn candy chocolate side up and mark in squares or rectangles (with a French chef's knife, if available). Tap back of knife with hammer to cut in pieces. Makes about 96 pieces, or 1¾ pounds.

NOTE: About ¼ c. of the chopped almonds may be reserved and sprinkled over the melted chocolate. These should be chopped finer than those used in the toffee.

Jellied Candies

Jellied Candies

The versatile performer in several unusual candies and confections is gelatin. There are two delights which we especially recommend: delicate Homemade Marshmallows, which mothers like to fix for their children; and the sparkling sweet that our taste-testers called "darling Candy Strawberries"—as fresh-tasting as they look. You can go fancy for a special party and buy marzipan strawberry leaves on (artificial) stems to stick in top of the candy berries, but we give you another choice for topknots for your "berries" too: almonds, tinted green. Tasty and pretty.

Among the candy recipes in other sections of this book which call for gelatin as an ingredient are: Christmas Cherry Fudge, Northwestern Apricot Candy and Northwestern Apple Candy. Do look them up in the Index.

Homemade Marshmallows

Light, delicate and delicious

2   tblsp. unflavored gelatin
¾   c. cold water
2   c. sugar
⅛   tsp. salt
¾   c. boiling water
1   tblsp. vanilla
Chopped nuts or toasted flaked coconut
        for coating

Soften gelatin in cold water 5 minutes; then dissolve by stirring over hot water.

Combine sugar, salt and boiling water in 2-qt. heavy saucepan; cook, stirring until sugar dissolves, to the soft crack stage (280°).

Pour into mixing bowl along with the gelatin mixture and beat at low speed for 3 minutes; continue beating at medium speed for 10 minutes or until mixture is fluffy and creamy. Add vanilla and pour into an 8″ square pan dusted with confectioners sugar.

Cool ½ hour or until set, then cut in 36 squares with knife moistened in water. Roll in nuts or coconut. Place in airtight container and put in refrigerator, freezer or other cold place until ready to use. Makes about 1 pound.

NOTE: Tint the gelatin mixture while heating—pale green, pink or yellow—if you wish. Roll green candy in chopped nuts, pink in flaked coconut, yellow in toasted coconut and white in nuts or coconut. You can vary the flavorings if you wish. Instead of vanilla use almond, peppermint, orange or lemon extract.

Candied Marshmallows

A children's party special that grownups also enjoy—try them

½ c. sugar
½ c. light corn syrup
½ c. smooth peanut butter
1 (4 oz.) pkg. marshmallows (16)

Combine sugar and corn syrup in 1-qt. heavy saucepan. Cook over medium heat, stirring constantly, until mixture comes to a boil and sugar is dissolved.

Remove from heat; stir in peanut butter until well blended.

With 2 forks, dip marshmallows, one at a time, into mixture until evenly coated. Place on buttered cake racks, set on waxed paper, to drain and cool. Makes 16.

Candy Strawberries

So sparkly, with a fresh strawberry taste

2 (3 oz.) pkgs. strawberry flavor gelatin
1 c. ground pecans
1 c. ground coconut
¾ c. sweetened condensed milk
½ tsp. vanilla
Red sugar crystals
Green food color
Slivered almonds

Mix together gelatin, pecans, coconut, condensed (not evaporated) milk and vanilla. Shape mixture into strawberries; chill at least 1 hour.

Roll chilled berries in sugar crystals.

Add food color to almonds to tint a delicate green. Use for leaves and stems of berries. Store in a cool place. Makes about 48 strawberries, depending on size, or 1 pound, 3 ounces.

After-Dinner Jellies

Instead of gelatin, liquid fruit pectin from the supermarket shelf sets these delightful jellied confections. The orange jellies in fluted chocolate cups make such a pretty picture that guests will start exclaiming whenever the confections appear. And after they sample the fresh orange taste, you'll hear how good the jellies are.

After-Dinner Jellies

Fluted chocolate cups hold orange-flavored jellied candy

½ oz. paraffin (2x1x½")
8 squares semisweet chocolate
     (8 oz. pkg.)
1 (6 oz.) bottle liquid fruit pectin
½ tsp. baking soda
1 c. sugar
1 c. light corn syrup
1 tsp. grated orange peel
1½ tsp. orange extract
Few drops red and yellow food color
3 tblsp. chopped nuts

Melt parafin and chocolate in top of double boiler over hot (not boiling) water; stir. With a small spatula, coat insides of thirty 1½" fluted paper cups with chocolate (keep chocolate over hot water while you work). Refrigerate until firm.

Pour pectin into a 2-qt. saucepan; stir in soda. (Pectin will foam.)

Mix sugar and corn syrup in another saucepan. Place both saucepans over highest heat. Cook mixtures, stirring alternately, until foam has disappeared from pectin mixture and sugar mixture is boiling rapidly, about 3 to 5 minutes.

Pour pectin mixture in stream into boiling sugar mixture, stirring constantly. Boil and stir for 1 minute.

Remove from heat, add orange peel, extract and food color. Spoon quickly into chocolate cups. Sprinkle with nuts. Refrigerate until firm. Store in covered pan in refrigerator. Peel off papers to serve. Makes 30 jellies.

NOTE: This treat is not recommended for packing and shipping.

Perfect Caramels

Chocolate Caramels

A thoughtful gift for the holidays—candy is rich and chewy

2½ c. white sugar
1 c. light corn syrup
1 c. water
1 c. light cream (or ½ c. heavy cream plus ½ c. dairy half-and-half)
1 c. butter (2 sticks)
3 squares unsweetened chocolate
1½ oz. piece paraffin (1½ x 1½ x ⅝" thick), cut in small pieces

Combine all ingredients in a 4-qt. heavy saucepan. Stir and cook over medium heat until sugar is dissolved and butter and paraffin melted. Reduce heat to low and cook, stirring occasionally, until mixture reaches 240°. This will take about 30 to 40 minutes. Continue to cook, stirring constantly and vigorously to prevent scorching, to the firm ball stage (248°). (The entire cooking period will be 50 to 60 minutes.)

Remove from heat at once and pour into a lightly buttered 9" square pan. When candy starts to get firm, mark in ¾" strips with a knife. When candy is cool and firm (about 3 hours), cut in strips with knife. Remove strips from pan, one at a time; place on cutting board and with sharp knife, cut in squares or rectangles. Wrap individually in waxed paper. Makes about 10 dozen caramels, or 2½ pounds.

Unforgettable Caramel Pecan Logs

You don't often taste homemade candy as luscious as Caramel Pecan Logs. This is one of the most praised treats our recipe testers have made. The Kansas FARM JOURNAL reader who first sent us the recipe says: "I've been making the logs for at least 15 years. They take more time than most candies, but they're worth every minute spent. I like to make the centers one day to refrigerate for cutting, dipping and rolling in nuts the next day."

Scarcely had we tested the recipe, when along came a letter from an Illinois homemaker with almost the same recipe. She wrote: "I'm eternally grateful to my sister-in-law, who gave me the recipe for Caramel Pecan Logs. Sometimes I roll the caramel-dipped logs in coconut instead of pecans. And for variety, I occasionally make chocolate nougat centers by adding 2 squares of unsweetened chocolate, melted with the butter."

Both of the champion makers of this superb candy offer the same important suggestion: Make this candy only if you have a candy thermometer.

This isn't a new recipe, but one of the tried and true treasures.

Caramel Pecan Logs

One of the best taste treats Santa could bring anyone for Christmas—our big recipe, just right for gifts

Nougat Center:
- 3 c. sugar
- 1⅓ c. light corn syrup
- 1 c. water
- 2 egg whites, stiffly beaten
- ¼ c. melted butter
- 1 tsp. vanilla
- ⅛ tsp. salt

Caramel Coating:
- 2 c. sugar
- 1¼ c. light corn syrup
- 1½ c. light cream
- 1 tsp. vanilla
- ¼ tsp. salt
- 1½ lbs. pecans, coarsely chopped (about 6 c.)

To make nougat center, combine ¾ c. sugar, ⅔ c. corn syrup and ¼ c. water in 1½-qt. heavy saucepan. Stir over medium heat until sugar dissolves; then boil to soft ball stage (238°).

Pour syrup over beaten egg whites, beating constantly until slightly cool; this takes about 5 minutes. Spoon into well-buttered bowl and make a well in the center. Let stand while you make the second syrup.

Combine remaining 2¼ c. sugar, ⅔ c. corn syrup and ¾ c. water. Cook over medium heat, stirring until sugar is dissolved. Continue cooking to the hard ball stage (258°).

Pour syrup immediately into center of egg white mixture in bowl. Beat vigorously with wooden spoon until thoroughly mixed. Stir in butter, vanilla and salt.

Let stand, beating occasionally, until mixture is very stiff and holds its shape. Transfer from bowl into waxed paper-lined 8″ square pan. With buttered fingers, press it into pan. Keep in the refrigerator until very firm—for 2 or 3 hours or days.

Turn the firm candy onto cutting board and remove waxed paper. Cut in half and then in half again, making 4 small squares. Cut each square into 4 logs of equal size; you'll have 16 small logs. You are now ready to make the caramel coating.

To make caramel coating, combine sugar, corn syrup and ½ c. cream in 2-qt. heavy saucepan. Stir over medium heat until sugar dissolves; cook to soft ball stage (236°).

Slowly add ½ c. cream and again cook to soft ball stage (236°). Add remaining ½ c. cream and cook mixture to firm ball stage (242°); stir often as caramel mixture thickens. Remove from heat and stir in vanilla and salt.

Pour mixture into top of double boiler and set over hot water. Gently drop nougat logs, one at a time, into caramel (work quickly with two forks), coating thoroughly; hold log over caramel to drain slightly. Drop logs into shallow dish containing nuts and roll to coat.

When cool, wrap logs in aluminum foil and store in refrigerator at least 5 hours, or for weeks. When ready to serve, cut in ½″ slices. Makes 4¾ pounds or about 128 slices.

Holiday Logs

Professional-looking, easy to make; logs make a hit when shared

⅓ c. soft butter or margarine
¼ c. light corn syrup
1 tsp. vanilla
½ tsp. salt
1 lb. confectioners sugar
Green food color
Few drops of oil of peppermint
Red food color
Few drops oil of cinnamon
Few drops rum extract
1 lb. caramels (light or dark)
3 tblsp. light cream or evaporated milk
1½ c. chopped pecans, toasted

To make fondant center, combine butter, syrup, vanilla and salt in a large mixing bowl. Add confectioners sugar; mix together with a fork, then knead with hands. Mixture will be very dry, but softens with kneading.

Divide in thirds. Knead on board, blending green color and oil of peppermint into one third, red food color and oil of cinnamon into another third and rum extract into last third. (Adjust flavorings to taste.)

Form into rolls 1″ in diameter. Cut fondant rolls in halves crosswise to make 6 rolls. Wrap individually in waxed paper and store overnight in freezer or refrigerator.

Make caramel-nut coating next day by heating caramels and cream in double boiler. Dip chilled fondant rolls into warm caramel mixture, spooning to cover. (Work quickly so rolls don't soften.) Immediately roll in chopped pecans; wrap in aluminum foil and chill. Store logs in refrigerator or freezer until ready to serve. Slice just before serving. Makes 2⅓ pounds.

Wonderful Oklahoma Brown Candy

You'll never put more delicious candy in your mouth than Oklahoma Brown Candy. The recipe for it originated in the Sooner State, where the candy is a favorite. Its color is a rich caramel brown and it's a first cousin of caramels. The superb flavor comes from the caramelized sugar and the generous amount of pecans, a native Oklahoma nut, embedded in the luscious sweetness. You can use half the amount of pecans if you wish, or you can use other kinds of nuts. But once you take the pecans out of Oklahoma Brown Candy you must delete Oklahoma from its name.

You may want a helper standing by, at least the first time you make this candy. The trick is to get the sugar caramelized and ready to pour at the same time the sugar-milk mixture reaches the boil. Also, it's helpful to have someone share the beating.

Some Oklahoma women use their pressure cooker kettles for the saucepan in which to cook the candy. The recipe makes a big batch, so a deep cooking pan is desirable. Sometimes they pour the candy into loaf pans and, when cold, remove it from the pans, wrap the loaves in foil or plastic wrap and store them in the refrigerator to cut in slices as they wish. This candy is an excellent keeper if wrapped and refrigerated. Or you can freeze it.

Oklahoma Brown Candy

Let's give thanks to the Sooners who invented this superlative candy

6   c. sugar
2   c. milk or dairy half-and-half
¼   tsp. baking soda
½   c. butter or margarine (1 stick)
1   tsp. vanilla
2   lbs. pecans, broken (about 8½ c.)

Combine 4 c. sugar and milk in 4-qt. heavy saucepan. Stir and set aside.

Put remaining 2 c. sugar in 10″ heavy skillet over medium heat. Stir constantly until sugar starts to melt. Then place sugar-milk mixture over low heat, stirring occasionally until sugar dissolves.

Continue melting sugar in skillet, stirring, until all is melted and is the color of light brown sugar. (Melting sugar scorches easily so watch carefully). This may take almost 30 minutes.

Pour melted sugar in a fine stream into the boiling sugar-milk mixture, stirring constantly. The secret to success is to pour it in a very fine stream.

Cook combined mixture to the firm ball stage (246°). Remove from heat at once. Stir Stir in baking soda. The mixture foams vigorously when soda is added. Add butter and let stand 30 minutes.

Add vanilla and beat with wooden spoon until mixture loses its gloss and begins to thicken. Add pecans, and stir to mix.

Pour into lightly buttered 13x9x2″ pan. Cool slightly and cut in pieces of the desired size. Makes 4½ to 5 pounds.

Caramel Apple Slices

Praline-like; spicy and sweet

2   c. white sugar
1   c. brown sugar, firmly packed
1   c. finely grated, peeled apples and juice
        (2 medium apples)
¾   c. evaporated milk
2   tblsp. butter or margarine
½   tsp. ground cinnamon
¼   tsp. salt
½   c. miniature marshmallows
1   c. chopped pecans or walnuts

Combine first 7 ingredients in 3-qt. heavy saucepan. Cook to soft ball stage (240°). Mixture scorches easily, so stir often. Without scraping saucepan, pour into buttered 13x9x2″ pan; cool at room temperature.

When completely cooled, divide candy in half. Pat each half into an 8x6″ rectangle on waxed paper. Place double row of marshmallows along one 8″ edge. Roll as for jelly roll; roll in chopped nuts. Repeat with other rectangle of candy.

Wrap in waxed paper. Chill until firm; then cut in ¼″ slices. Store in airtight container. Makes 3 dozen ¼″ slices.

NOTE: This candy is not recommended for packaging and shipping.

Caramel Mallow Roll-Up

Candy, marshmallows and walnuts—the young crowd likes this

½ lb. light caramels (28)
¼ c. dairy half-and-half
2 tblsp. butter
2 c. confectioners sugar, sifted
17 regular marshmallows
¾ c. finely chopped walnuts

Combine caramels, half-and-half and butter in 1½-qt. heavy saucepan. Place over heat and stir until caramels are melted. Stir in confectioners sugar. Remove from heat.

Spread caramel mixture on buttered waxed paper to make a 16x5″ rectangle.

Place marshmallows, end to end, along one side of rectangle. Roll up, starting with marshmallow side, by lifting with waxed paper.

Spread nuts on waxed paper; coat roll with them. Wrap in waxed paper. Chill several hours. To serve, cut in ½″ slices. Makes 1 (16″) log, or about 32 pieces.

Candy Turtles

Spread turtles on tray—they're eye openers and make candy-talk

½ lb. soft caramels (25)
2 tblsp. heavy cream
1¼ c. pecan halves (about)
4 squares semisweet chocolate

Melt caramels with cream over hot water. Let cool about 10 minutes.

Arrange pecan halves in groups of three on lightly greased baking sheet (one for head of turtle and two for legs).

Spoon melted caramels over nuts, leaving tips showing. Let stand at least 30 minutes.

Melt chocolate over hot water. Remove from water and stir until smooth. Cool; spread over caramel of turtles (do not cover nut tips). Makes 24 turtles.

Try a Taffy Pull

Try a Taffy Pull

It takes pull to make taffy, but the experience —and results—are worth the time and effort. Sharing the work and eating pleasure with family or friends on a winter day, when you want to stay indoors, gives you an understanding of how much fun the old-fashioned candy pull brought to country homes.

An Indiana mother is reviving the old custom. She writes: "My two children, 10 and 12 years, were so restless one afternoon last winter when we were snowbound, that I decided to show them how to make and pull taffy. A few weeks later they asked to invite three friends over for a Friday evening taffy pull. I helped them cook the candy and then left the kitchen. Sounds of merriment proved they liked the pulling—and tasting."

"We plan to have another taffy party. I really think our kitchen is the most cheerful and prettiest room in the house. This is a good way to entertain there."

For success with taffy, try one of the recipes that follow. If the candy should get sugary, put it in a saucepan with 2 tblsp. corn syrup and ¾ c. water. Cook it over low heat, stirring constantly until the taffy dissolves. Then cook it as the recipe directs.

How to Pull Taffy

Turn the cooked, hot candy into a buttered shallow pan or large buttered platter. Turn the edges to the center with a heavy spatula. This encourages even cooling.

Start pulling as soon as taffy is cool enough to handle. If it gets too cool to pull easily, warm it a few minutes in a moderate oven (350°).

Pull with tips of fingers and thumbs. If candy sticks, dip fingertips in cornstarch. Some candy makers prefer to butter their fingers lightly.

Pull candy slowly until hands are about 18″ apart. Fold half of candy back on other half and continue pulling and folding until taffy gets hard to pull. (Some of our recipes indicate how taffy looks at this stage.)

Divide pulled candy in thirds or fourths; work with one part at a time. With one end of candy on a buttered surface or a surface dusted with confectioners sugar, stretch taffy to make a rope from ½ to ¾″ thick. Repeat with other portions of pulled taffy. Some candy makers prefer to twist the ropes even though the taffy is less fluffy than when untwisted. (Twisting removes the small airholes.)

Cut the ropes in bite-size pieces with buttered scissors. Cut one piece, then turn the rope of taffy halfway over and cut another piece. Continue cutting and turning.

Let pieces fall separately onto a surface that has been buttered or dusted with confectioners sugar. When cold, wrap pieces individually in waxed paper; if desired, place in airtight containers and put in freezer or refrigerator. Wrapping pieces of taffy individually in waxed paper makes it keep better, but it may be stored successfully unwrapped in airtight containers in refrigerator or freezer.

Foolproof Vanilla Taffy

Both cinnamon and vanilla taffy are good. Which will you make?

    3   c. sugar
    2   c. less 2 tblsp. light corn syrup
    1   c. water
    2   tblsp. butter
    1   tsp. vanilla

Butter sides of a 3-qt. heavy saucepan; add sugar, corn syrup and water. Stir with a wooden spoon until sugar dissolves. Bring to a boil quickly over medium-heat. Stir as little as possible and do not scrape sides of pan above cooking mixture (to prevent sugar crystals forming). If sugar crystals form on sides of pan, wipe them off. Cook to the hard ball stage (256°).

Add butter and continue cooking to 262°. Remove from heat. Pour into buttered and chilled shallow pan or platter (about 13x9"); turn edges to center with heavy spatula. While candy cools, make several gashes on surface; add vanilla (to be worked in during pulling).

When candy is cool enough to handle, pull until taffy changes to a shiny platinum ribbon (see directions for How to Pull Taffy).

Cut in bite-size pieces with buttered scissors. Cool, then wrap pieces individually in waxed paper. Store in airtight containers. Makes 2½ pounds.

VARIATION

Cinnamon Taffy: Instead of vanilla, add 6 to 8 drops oil of cinnamon while taffy is cooling, kneading candy with a spatula at first, then with hands before dividing and pulling.

Creamy Walnut Taffy

Gelatin and cream are the unusual ingredients in this new taffy. It gets creamy and improves as it stands

    ½   tsp. unflavored gelatin
    ¼   c. cold water
    2   c. sugar
    1   c. light cream (or ½ c. heavy cream plus
            ½ c. dairy half-and-half)
    1   c. light corn syrup
    2   tsp. melted paraffin
    ¼   tsp. baking soda
    ½   c. finely chopped walnuts
    1   tsp. vanilla

Soften gelatin in cold water.

Combine sugar, cream, corn syrup, paraffin and softened gelatin in 2-qt. heavy saucepan; stir to dissolve sugar. Quickly bring to a boil over medium-high heat and cook, stirring as little as possible, to the hard ball stage (256°). Continue cooking to 262°.

Remove from heat; add soda, nuts and vanilla, and stir to combine. Pour into buttered shallow pan or platter (about 13x9"). Turn edges to center with heavy spatula.

When candy is cool enough to handle, pull until taffy takes on an opaque look (see directions for How to Pull Taffy). Cut in bite-size pieces with buttered scissors. Cool, then wrap pieces individually in waxed paper; store in airtight containers. Makes 2 pounds.

Old-Fashioned Molasses Taffy

Reminds grandparents of taffy-pulling fun on wintery evenings

2   c. molasses
1   c. sugar
2   tblsp. butter
1   tblsp. vinegar

Combine ingredients in a 3-qt. heavy saucepan. Stir with a wooden spoon until sugar is dissolved; bring to a boil over medium heat. If mixture foams during cooking, stir around the outside under the cooking surface and if excessive, reduce heat to medium-low. Continue to cook to the hard ball stage (260°).

Pour taffy into a large (about 13x9″) buttered and chilled shallow pan or platter (do not scrape cooking pan). Turn edges to center with heavy spatula.

When candy is cool enough to handle, pull until taffy is light in color and hard to pull (see directions for How to Pull Taffy). Cut in bite-size pieces with buttered scissors. Cool, then wrap pieces individually in waxed paper; store in airtight containers. Makes 1¾ pounds.

VARIATION

Peppermint Molasses Taffy: While taffy is cooling, add 4 to 5 drops oil of peppermint; work it into the candy as you pull. Candy has a delicious flavor.

Peppermint Taffy Sticks

The pink of perfection in taffy

2   c. sugar
½   c. light corn syrup
⅔   c. water
5   drops red food color
¼   tsp. oil of peppermint

Combine sugar, corn syrup and water in 2-qt. heavy saucepan. Stir over low heat until sugar is dissolved. Add food color to tint a delicate pink and cook without stirring to the hard ball stage (265°).

Remove from heat and add oil of peppermint.

Pour into buttered shallow pan (about 13x9″) or onto buttered platter. When cool enough to handle, pull until light and fluffy (see directions for How to Pull Taffy). Quickly stretch in thin ropes and twist around oiled 4½″ wooden lollipop sticks (from meat counter). When set, slip taffy from sticks and wrap coils individually in waxed paper. Place in airtight container and store in a cool place. To serve, remove waxed paper wrappings. Makes about 1¼ pounds.

NOTE: You can stretch part or all of pulled taffy into ropes and cut in pieces as with any taffy. Wrap each piece in waxed paper, twisting paper ends.

Salt Water Taffy

You can divide taffy, tinting and flavoring each portion differently

```
2    c. sugar
1    c. light corn syrup
1½   c. water
1½   tsp. salt
2    tsp. glycerin
2    tblsp. butter
2    tsp. vanilla
```

Combine sugar, syrup, water, salt and glycerin in a 3-qt. heavy saucepan. Place on low heat and stir until sugar dissolves. Then cook without stirring to the hard ball stage (260°).

Remove from heat and add butter. When butter is melted, pour into a buttered shallow pan (about 13x9″).

When cool enough to handle, gather into a ball and pull until rather firm. Add vanilla while pulling. Stretch out into a long rope and cut in 1 or 2″ pieces. Wrap each piece in waxed paper when hard; twist paper at both ends. This will keep candy from becoming sticky. Makes about 1¼ pounds.

NOTE: You can tint the taffy while pulling it. Different flavors may be added, also in the pulling, instead of the vanilla. Pink taffy usually is flavored with wintergreen, white with vanilla, green with spearmint.

Pulled Mints

You pull this like taffy, getting mints that melt in your mouth

```
2    c. sugar
1    c. water
¼    c. butter or margarine (½ stick)
Pinch cream of tartar
Few drops food color (your choice)
4    to 5 drops oil of peppermint or
     wintergreen, lemon or cinnamon
```

Combine sugar, water, butter and cream of tartar in 2-qt. heavy saucepan. Stir over medium heat until sugar is completely dissolved.

Cook, without stirring, over high heat until mixture reaches the hard ball stage (260°). If sugar crystals form on sides of pan, wipe them off.

Pour onto buttered marble slab or buttered large shallow pan or platter. With buttered hands, turn edges into center so they won't get hard. Let cool.

When cool enough to handle, sprinkle over drops of food color and your choice of flavor. Pick up into a ball. Hold in one hand, pull out with other hand; fold back and pull again, working in color and flavoring (see directions for How to Pull Taffy). Turn, to pull all parts evenly. Continue pulling until almost cold.

Stretch out in a "ribbon" of even thickness (about ½" to ¾" wide). Cut off with kitchen shears in short lengths. Store in airtight container with waxed paper between layers. Makes about 1 pound.

Tempting

Bark Candy

Toasted Almond Bark

Creamy candy with toasted almonds is easy to make and extra-good

2 c. sugar
⅔ c. milk
1 tblsp. light corn syrup
¼ tsp. salt
2 tblsp. butter
1 tsp. vanilla
1 c. toasted unblanched almonds

Combine sugar, milk, corn syrup and salt in 2-qt. heavy saucepan. Cook, stirring constantly until sugar dissolves and mixture comes to a boil. Then cook without stirring to soft ball stage (234°).

Remove from heat; add butter, but do not stir. Let cool until lukewarm (110°). Then add vanilla. Beat until mixture thickens and is creamy. Add toasted almonds. Then spread about ½" thick on wax paper-lined baking sheet. Cool; break in pieces. Makes about 1½ pounds.

Dipped Pretzels

White-coated pretzels are crunchy and tasty —and toasted almonds in bark candy are a bonus sure to please everyone

1 lb. white confection coating
24 small pretzels

Cut coating in small pieces; place in double boiler over boiling water. Stir constantly until it is melted.

Cool until coating is 105° on candy thermometer. Set it over warm water of the same temperature.

Dip pretzels, one at a time, into melted coating to cover them. Place on waxed paper to dry. Use remaining coating to make Almond Bark.

NOTE: Unsalted pretzels will keep longer than the salted kind, but salted ones may be used.

Almond Bark: Add ¼ tsp. almond extract to remaining melted coating. Stir to mix, and stir in ½ c. unblanched almonds. Pour onto waxed paper. Let cool, then break in pieces. Makes 3 to 4 dozen pieces.

Hard Candies

Hard Candies
Crystal-Clear and Color-Bright

When the weather-watcher in the country family steps outdoors to look at the sky before retiring and comes in predicting a fair, dry tomorrow, candy makers take notice; especially if you want to make hard candies, since they have a remarkable affinity for water—absorb it from the air and quickly become sticky. The first step to success in making hard candy is choosing a fair day low in humidity.

You want hard candies crystal-clear and color-bright. So you have to try to prevent sugar crystals from forming; they affect both clearness and color. Here are ways to avoid crystallization:

Include corn syrup with the sugar and liquid in the saucepan—that is, choose a recipe that contains the syrup. Ours do!

When you put it on to cook, stir the candy mixture until the sugar dissolves; then refrain from stirring during the remainder of the cooking. Keep it at a steady, fairly low boil.

Remove any sugar crystals that form by wiping sides of saucepan with a damp, cloth-covered fork or pastry brush.

The cooking syrup tends to darken toward the end of the cooking. This dulls the color when you tint the candy. One way to prevent darkening is to cook the candy in a saucepan with deep, straight sides so there is a relatively small cooking surface. In some of our tests we used the top of a large double boiler, which is ideal in shape (rounded bottom) and size. It also helps, when the temperature reaches 280°, to lower the heat for the remainder of the cooking.

Add the flavoring and food color as soon as the candy is cooked, first removing it from the heat. Oil flavorings are desirable because they are strong. You may think you are adding a lot, but some of the flavor "goes up in smoke," or evaporates. That's what gives the kitchen such an enchanting aroma. Paste food color is a favorite for hard candies. You dissolve it in very little water before adding it to the candy. Stir the coloring and flavoring into the candy just enough to mix. Too much stirring may produce sugar crystals.

These candies deserve their name because they harden quickly. You have to work fast once the cooking ends. If you pour the candy into an oiled pan to cool, stand by to mark it in pieces just as soon as it cools enough to hold an impression. The candy will still feel warm. Score the candy in strips, first one direction, then across, to mark it in pieces. Use a sharp, strong knife, working the knife back and forth to make an impression—but do not cut through the candy.

When the candy is cold, turn the pan over on counter top or cutting board and give it a tap. The candy will fall out. Break it in pieces along the lines made with the knife. Store candy in airtight containers with waxed paper between the layers, or wrap each piece individually in waxed paper or plastic wrap. Put in a cool place. Unless the pieces are individually wrapped, don't box hard candy with other kinds of candy. (Hard candies rob other candies of their moisture—the hard candies will become sticky and the other ones will dry out.)

Fascinating Lollypops

Lollypops shaped like roosters, squirrels and deer got a Michigan mother involved in the candy business. She took some of the lollypops she makes for her seven children to a food bazaar. They not only sold quickly, but people telephoned her and came to her door asking her to make and sell animal lollypops for them to give to their children and grandchildren. The pleas were so sincere that she yielded and now, every year starting at Halloween and continuing up to the Christmas holidays, she makes and sells lollypops.

She shapes them with heavy, cast metal molds. These are not easily found and are rather expensive (but a good investment for her). An imaginative mother in the West, unable to find molds, substitutes cookie cutters *open* at both top and bottom. A good way to display lollypops at a food sale is to insert the stick ends in a large circle of Styrofoam.

Increase the amount of oil flavorings if you like a more pronounced flavor. The smaller children on our taste panel preferred ⅛ tsp. oil of peppermint, for instance, while adults liked ¼ tsp. And do use different flavors and food colors. Here are a few suggestions: oil of lime or spearmint with green food color, oil of wintergreen with pink, oil of lemon with yellow, oil of orange with orange, and oil of peppermint or oil of cinnamon with red.

Lollypops

Children do talk to the animals when they're candy on sticks

2	c. sugar
⅔	c. light corn syrup
1	c. water
⅛	tsp. salt
⅛	tsp. oil of peppermint
¼	tsp. red food color

Oil inside of small cookie cutters that are open at both top and bottom; select cutters in the shape of animals, such as a chicken, rabbit, squirrel or other animals children like, or in the shape of a Christmas tree or star, etc. Place about 4″ apart on oiled baking sheets or oiled aluminum foil.

Combine sugar, corn syrup, water and salt in 2-qt. heavy saucepan. Place over medium heat, stirring constantly until sugar dissolves and mixture comes to a boil. If sugar crystals form on sides of pan, wipe them off.

Reduce heat and cook at a steady, fairly low boil without stirring until candy mixture reaches the hard crack stage (310°).

Remove from heat; add oil of peppermint and food color. Stir only enough to mix.

Quickly pour hot candy mixture, without scraping pan, into cookie cutters. Candy should be about ¼″ thick. As soon as candy is set and while still warm, remove cutters and twist a lollypop stick (wooden meat skewer) into each candy. With broad spatula, loosen lollypops from baking sheet before they cool.

Repeat until all candy syrup is used. If it gets too hard to pour, stir over low heat just enough to melt candy. Work fast.

Wrap individually in waxed paper as soon as cool to prevent candy from absorbing moisture and becoming sticky. Store in airtight boxes. Makes about 30 lollypops, depending on size of cookie cutters used.

VARIATIONS

Lollypop Faces: Instead of pouring cooked lollypop mixture into cookie cutters, drop it from tip of teaspoon or tablespoon, depending on size of lollypops desired. Drop each spoonful over one end of a lollypop stick on oiled baking sheet. (Arrange sticks 4 to 5″ apart on baking sheet before starting to cook candy.) When cool, outline a face and features on each lollypop by piping on confectioners sugar frosting (confectioners sugar and water), tinted if you like. Makes about 15 to 20 large lollypops.

Halloween Lollypops: Drop out lollypop mixture in circles or disks onto sticks as for Lollypop Faces. Press candy corn in any design desired on lollypops before they cool; they'll not adhere if candy gets too cool.

Hard Candy Squares: Prepare candy as for Lollypops, but pour it immediately when it reaches 310° into a greased or oiled 8″ square pan. Cool just until surface of candy will hold an impression. Then mark with sharp pointed knife into squares; mark lengthwise, let set a few minutes, then mark crosswise. When candy is cold, turn pan unside down over broad or table top. Tap pan sharply to remove candy. Break pieces apart. Makes 64 pieces.

Anise Candy

Candy is a clear, sparkling red—attractive served on milk glass

2 c. sugar
1 c. light corn syrup
½ c. water
¼ tsp. red food color
1 tsp. oil of anise

Combine sugar, corn syrup and water in 2-qt. heavy saucepan. Stir well and cook over low heat, stirring until sugar dissolves.

Continue cooking at a fairly low boil, without stirring, to the soft crack stage (280°). If sugar crystals form on sides of pan, wipe them off. (Cook slowly during the last few minutes to avoid darkening of candy syrup.)

Remove from heat; add food color and oil of anise, stirring no more than necessary to mix.

Pour into an oiled 13x9x2″ pan. Candy should be in a thin layer. As it starts to cool, mark with knife in bite-size pieces. Keep scoring pieces with knife until they hold their shape.

Cool completely; remove from pan and wipe any excess oil from block of candy. Break in pieces. Place in airtight container with waxed paper between layers and store in a cool place. Makes about 130 pieces or 1½ pounds.

Colorful Old-Fashioned Hard Candy

Fill a fancy glass or apothecary jar with peppermint-flavored Old-Fashioned Hard Candy, tinted green, and a twin container with cinnamon-flavored candy, tinted red. You'll have a sweet Christmas gift the older generation especially enjoys. Or fill little plastic bags with the candy in different colors and flavors for the holiday bazaar. "I've taken this candy in small plastic bags to food sales," says the California woman who shares her recipe. "It sells well," she adds, "especially to people who bought it at previous sales." In other words, demand increases when customers get acquainted with the candy.

The trick in making this candy is to cut it while warm. This is what the contributor of the recipe says: "I keep a pair of white cotton gloves on hand to wear when I make this candy. They make it possible for me to start cutting sooner (I learned by experience). At first I decided to let the candy cool and then break it into pieces. It looked like broken glass and no one wanted to eat it. The ideal situation is for one person to cut the candy in strips and another to snip it with scissors into pieces, because it hardens fast."

Here's another tip from the California candy maker: "I keep a saucepan partly filled with hot water on the range. If the candy begins to cool faster than I can cut it, I set the pan of candy over the saucepan of hot water. If the candy starts to get sticky, I move it back to the work counter."

You can buy the oil flavorings at drugstores, but tell the druggist you want to use them in cooking.

Old-Fashioned Hard Candy

Here's a slow-eating, colorful gift—Pleases Grandpa and grandkids

2 c. sugar
1 c. water
¾ c. light corn syrup
Food color (red, green, yellow, etc.)
½ tsp. oil of cinnamon, clove, peppermint, wintergreen or anise
Confectioners sugar

Combine sugar, water and corn syrup in 2-qt. heavy saucepan. Cook, stirring constantly until sugar is dissolved; then cook without stirring, lowering heat and cooking more slowly during the last few minutes, to the hard crack stage (300°). If sugar crystals form on sides of pan, wipe them off.

Remove from heat; add food color and oil flavoring, stirring only enough to mix. Pour into 2 well-buttered 9" pie pans. Set one pan of candy over a saucepan containing hot water. As soon as the other pan of candy is cool enough to touch, cut it with scissors into strips 1" wide, then snip strips into pieces. Work fast. Drop pieces onto a buttered baking sheet. If candy cools too quickly, set it on saucepan over hot water to soften it, but if it gets sticky, return at once to work counter. Repeat with second pan of candy.

When candy is cool, sprinkle with confectioners sugar. Store in airtight containers with waxed paper between the layers. Makes about 100 pieces or 1¼ pounds.

"Stained Glass" Hard Candy

Use these candies to trim the tree, decorate a doorway or window

5   or 6 foil molds
2   c. sugar
⅓   c. light corn syrup
⅓   c. water
2   tblsp. vinegar
Few drops oil of peppermint
Food color

Cut aluminum foil in shapes of stars, bells and trees. Grease foil lightly with salad oil. Fold up edges to make ½″ sides. Seal corners with freezer tape to prevent leaks.

Combine sugar, syrup, water and vinegar in 2-qt. heavy saucepan. Cook, stirring constantly until sugar is dissolved; then cook without stirring, to the hard crack stage (300°). Remove from heat, stir in flavoring and color; cool *slightly.*

Pour colored candy into molds, about ⅛″ deep; spoon to cover bottom. When candy begins to set (before it hardens) use skewer to make holes for hanging. Allow candy to harden thoroughly; remove foil. Thread with ribbon or cord to hang. (Or you may pour the candy onto greased cookie sheet to make free-form shapes.) If candy becomes too firm to pour and shape, remelt over low heat (do not boil).

Tips: Try unusual combinations: Swirl food color through uncolored candy with a toothpick just after pouring it into molds; make molded candies of one color and dribble with a second color to get an elegant "stained glass" effect. Make small candies for hanging on a Christmas tree, larger ones for other decorations. Cover candy ornaments with plastic wrap and store in covered container at room temperature in a *dry* place; keep flat to prevent warping.

Other Hard Candies

Not all hard candies are clear. Three delicious examples with deeper color are Peppermint Drops with Chocolate, Sweedish Hard Candy and Swedish Toffee. Once you taste these treats, it's easy to understand why they are popular in Sweden. If you want to make candy that is different and distinctive, do try the recipes. You'll reap compliments on the candies and will have requests for recipes to use in making them.

Peppermint Drops with Chocolate

Tiny snowdrop peppermint candies wear chocolate topknots

1⅓   c. sugar
½   c. water
1   tsp. glycerin
2   drops oil of peppermint
2   squares semisweet chocolate

Combine sugar and water in 2-qt. heavy saucepan. Cook slowly, stirring constantly, until sugar is dissolved. When sugar is dissolved, remove spoon and do not stir again. Cook until candy reaches a boil, then blend in glycerin. Cover saucepan for 3 minutes. Uncover and cook at a fairly low boil to the soft ball stage (240°).

Remove from heat. Add oil of peppermint, stirring no more than necessary to mix. Pour onto oiled baking sheet. Work with oiled knife or spatula (as for fondant [see Index]) until candy is smooth and creamy.

Roll quickly into ¾″ balls; flatten with knife. Place on oiled baking sheet.

Melt chocolate and drop on top center of peppermint candies. Makes 32 candies, or ½ pound.

Swedish Hard Candy

This brittle, hard candy has a rich, delicious caramel-almond flavor

    1   c. sugar
    1   c. dark corn syrup
    ⅓   c. butter
    1   c. dairy half-and-half
    1   c. chopped blanched almonds

Combine sugar, corn syrup, butter and dairy half-and-half in 2-qt. heavy saucepan. Cook over low heat, stirring until sugar dissolves. (Watch carefully for mixture rises high in saucepan.) Continue cooking, stirring occasionally, to the hard ball stage (250°).

Remove from heat; add chopped almonds. Pour into small fluted paper dessert cups (1½″ in diameter at bottom), or drop from teaspoon onto waxed paper to make patties. Makes 54 to 60 patties, depending on size, or 1½ pounds.

NOTE: If you remove candy from paper cups, the patties will have fluted edges.

Swedish Toffee

This is different from our toffees—it's hard with a chocolate flavor

    2½   c. sugar
    1½   c. dark corn syrup
    ¼   c. cocoa
    1   c. heavy cream
    1   c. dairy half-and-half
    6   tblsp. butter
    1½   tsp. vanilla

Combine sugar, corn syrup, cocoa, cream, dairy half-and-half and 3 tblsp. butter in 3-qt. heavy saucepan. Cook over low heat, stirring until sugar dissolves. Continue cooking, stirring no more than necessary, to the hard ball stage (250°). Watch carefully, for mixture may boil to the top of saucepan.

Remove from heat; stir in remaining 3 tblsp. butter and vanilla. Pour into buttered 9″ square pan to cool.

While still warm, mark in 1″ squares; when cool, cut with a sharp knife and wrap individually in waxed paper. Makes 81 squares, or 2 pounds.

No Cook Candies

No-Cook Candies

There are some excellent candies that do not require cooking. In this section, we present several favorites. You'll note that a few of them call for melting chocolate in the top of a double boiler, or warming nuts in the oven or, in the recipe for our own homemade Almond Paste, the cooking of the flour-milk mixture. But beyond that, the mixtures are not cooked. And the candies that result are delicious, even spectacular! You'll find some party specials among the recipes that follow.

There are a number of no-cook recipes for fudge in this book, too: Double Boiler Fudge, Cream Cheese Fudge, White Almond Fudge and Cheddar Cheese Fudge. You'll find them all listed in the Index.

Almond Wreath for Happy Occasions

If you're looking for a different, delicious and beautiful sweet to serve to guests or to carry to special friends for a holiday gift, end your search. Make an Almond Wreath. We imported the recipe for it from a Swedish home economist now living in Holland. Our taste panel actually raved about the way this candy looks and tastes.

European women can buy almond paste to make this and other candies and confections. It's not available in very many of our markets; however, you'll find this homemade version easy to make and it costs much less than the commercial kind. You can adjust the amount of almond extract to suit your taste. Some people think ½ tsp. is just right, while others prefer the candy flavored with 1 tsp. of the extract.

You can decorate the chocolate-coated wreath as elaborately or as simply as your time and inclination dictate. We scattered some of the nuts and candied cherries we had on hand over it and everyone who saw the wreath spoke of how pretty it was.

The compliments continued when we cut the candy—each slice showed its pale pink, delicate green and soft chocolate sections. The flavor blend is superb. If you want to make a showy production, do the slicing with guests looking on, eagerly anticipating a chance to eat the candy.

Be sure also to make Orange/Chocolate Roll, a variation of Almond Wreath. The light chocolate-brown center surrounds a cream-colored orange candy. You coat the candy roll with chocolate. This sweet also is an adventure in good eating.

Almond Paste

This is the basic ingredient in three recipes that follow

½ c. flour
⅔ c. dairy half-and-half
¾ c. (about) blanched almonds (¼ lb.)
½ to 1 tsp. almond extract
1 lb. confectioners sugar (about)

In 1-qt. heavy saucepan, beat flour into dairy half-and-half. Place over medium heat, beating constantly with spoon until mixture gathers in one big lump. Remove from heat and scrape mixture onto a large cutting board. Work with table knife to keep it smooth while it cools.

In the meantime, grind almonds. You will have 1 cup.

When dough is cold, work in almonds and almond extract. In the beginning, it is easiest to work with a knife, but later, put it in bowl and mix with the hands, kneading it like dough. Work in enough confectioners sugar to make a mixture that is smooth and does not stick. The amount of confectioners sugar needed varies with the weather, but work mixture, adding sugar, until it can be handled and rolled with ease. You may need a little more than 1 lb. confectioners sugar. Makes 1½ pounds.

Almond Wreath

For a high point in feasting serve this candy at a holiday open house

1 recipe Almond Paste
1 tsp. cocoa
¼ c. finely chopped walnuts
1 drop red food color
1 tblsp. finely chopped candied cherries
1 drop green food color
2 tblsp. finely chopped pistachio nuts
5 squares semisweet chocolate, melted
Decorations for wreath (nuts, candied cherries, etc.)

Divide Almond Paste in 3 equal parts.

To one part, add cocoa to make a light brown; work in walnuts. Roll out to make a rope about 20″ long and ¾″ in diameter.

Add red food color to tint the second part a light pink. Work in finely chopped candied cherries. Roll to make a rope about ¾″ in diameter.

Add green food color to tint the second part a light pale green and work in pistachio nuts. Roll to make a rope the same size as first two parts.

Place first two rolls side by side on waxed paper and brush sides where they touch with melted chocolate to hold them together. Place green part on top over place where the first and second parts join. Shape gently in circle to make a wreath.

Spread wreath with remaining melted chocolate to cover completely. Decorate with additional walnuts and candied cherries, or as desired. Makes wreath with a diameter about 8½″

Let cool. To serve, cut in thin slices. Makes 2 pounds.

VARIATION

Orange/Chocolate Roll: Divide 1 recipe Almond Paste in half. Tint one half with 1 tsp. cocoa and work in ⅓ c. chopped walnuts. Shape into a roll about 1″ in diameter, 15½″ long. Add a little confectioners sugar if necessary to prevent sticking when shaping roll.

Work 1 tsp. finely grated orange peel into second half of Almond Paste. Flatten it by rolling with rolling pin, using confectioners sugar to prevent sticking, to make a narrow piece. Place chocolate roll on top of orange strip. Then roll orange candy around the chocolate candy, sealing it by pressing seam gently with fingers. Spread with 5 squares semisweet chocolate, melted, and garnish with chopped nuts. To serve, cut in thin slices. Makes 1 roll, about 1½″ in diameter and 17½ to 18″ long, or 2 pounds.

Party-Time Dutch Treats

Once you've made Almond Paste (for an Almond Wreath) and found out how easy it is to fix, how good it tastes and how inexpensive it is, you'll want to fix these handsome Dutch Treats. On a tray at a tea party or open house, they'll steal the show. They're real beauties—and so delectable.

The confections are actually nut macaroons topped with balls of Almond Paste and shiny Fondant Frosting, delicately tinted. You need not add other decorations, but silver dragees and chopped candied cherries give them a holiday look. You and your guests will be grateful for our neighbors in Holland who invented Dutch Treats.

Dutch Treats

Nut macaroons look like wee hats with brown brims; shiny pastel crowns are Fondant Frosting over Almond Paste

1 egg, separated
½ c. sugar
¾ c. ground pecans
Fondant Frosting
½ recipe Almond Paste (see Index)
Decorations (silver dragees, chopped
        candied cherries, nuts, etc.)

Combine egg yolk and sugar in small mixing bowl; beat until well blended. Stir in pecans and chill until mixture is slightly firm.

Beat egg white until it holds stiff, but not dry peaks. Fold into pecan mixture.

Drop mixture from teaspoon onto greased and lightly floured baking sheet. (Confections should be very small, about the size of a cherry.)

Bake in preheated slow oven (325°) 8 to 12 minutes, or until lightly browned. Remove from baking sheet and cool on wire racks.

Drop a little Fondant Frosting on centers of cool confections, making half of them green, the other half pink. Place a small ball (size of a cranberry) of Almond Paste on top of each confection.

Dribble on Fondant Frosting to cover Almond Paste balls. Garnish green-frosted confections with silver dragees and pink-frosted ones with finely chopped candied cherries. Makes 45 to 50 confections, or about 1 pound.

Fondant Frosting

It's a glassy-like fondant candy

1   c. plus 6 tblsp. sugar
Dash salt
⅛   tsp. cream of tartar
¾   c. water
1½ to 1¾ c. sifted confectioners sugar
¼   tsp. vanilla
2   to 3 drops red food color
2   to 3 drops green food color

Combine sugar, salt, cream of tartar and water in 1-qt. heavy saucepan. Cook over low heat, stirring constantly until sugar is dissolved. Then raise heat slightly and cook to 225° on candy thermometer. Remove from heat and cool to lukewarm (110°).

Place saucepan of frosting in pan of warm water and beat in confectioners sugar with wooden spoon. Add vanilla and continue to beat, adding confectioners sugar until frosting is thick and coats a metal spoon.

Remove half of frosting to bowl and tint a delicate pink with red food color. Tint remaining half of frosting with green food color.

Set saucepan and bowl of frosting in warm water so frosting will not get too thick. (If it gets too thick, add a few drops of warm water.) Dribble pink frosting over half of Dutch Treats, green frosting over remaining treats.

NOTE: To leftover Almond Paste, add ½ tsp. cocoa and 2 tblsp. finely chopped walnuts. Shape in ovals for a delicious candy. Or if you prefer, add ¼ tsp. grated orange peel to leftover Almond Paste and shape in ovals, or as desired. In Holland, where Dutch Treats rate highly, ground filberts or hazel nuts are used instead of ground pecans.

Decorative Party Treat Candy

Let imagination be your guide when you make pretty No-Cook Party Treat candy, but select the right kind of weather. Start with a fair day with low humidity. When it's humid the candies are slow to dry.

Mold the pieces in your hands to whatever shape you like, or go fancy and put the kneaded candy through your pastry tube or cookie press.

Vary the flavorings. The almond and vanilla extract combination is just one suggestion.

Tint the candy as you like, but in subtle shades. We divided the candy in half, tinted one part pale pink, the other green. You can make your own distinctive colors by blending drops of two or more food colors—red and yellow, for instance. Or leave the candy white.

Decorate the shaped candies if you wish. Roll them in flaked coconut, chopped nuts or grated chocolate. Or dip them in melted semi-sweet chocolate or confection coating.

Make the candies at least a day or two before the party. This allows ample time for them to set and frees you from bothering with them on party day.

No-Cook Party Treat

The big surprise is that this fancy candy is so easy to make

1   egg white
2   tsp. dairy half-and-half
⅛   tsp. almond extract
1   tsp. vanilla
¼   tsp. salt

1   lb. confectioners sugar
¼   c. butter or margarine
      (½ stick), melted
2   drops food color

Combine egg white, half-and-half, almond extract and vanilla in small mixing bowl. Stir salt and half the sugar into mixture. Add butter and food color. Gradually stir in remaining sugar until the desired consistency is reached.

Knead until smooth. Mold into desired shapes. Place on waxed paper and let dry. Store in airtight container in refrigerator or freezer. Makes about 1 pound.

Open House Mints

Ideal mints for holiday entertaining, wedding receptions, parties

2   tblsp. butter
2   tblsp. vegetable shortening
3   tblsp. warm water
5   c. sifted confectioners sugar
2   drops red food color
3   tsp. warm water
⅛   tsp. oil of cinnamon
2   drops green food color
⅛   tsp. oil of peppermint
2   drops yellow food color
⅛   tsp. oil of lemon

Combine butter, shortening, 2 tblsp. warm water and 2 c. confectioners sugar. Mix thoroughly.

Add remaining 3 c. confectioners sugar and 1 tblsp. warm water (if necessary, add 1 or more tblsp. confectioners sugar to make mix-ture stiff enough to roll out).

Divide mixture in thirds. To one third add red food color, mixed with 1 tsp. warm water and oil of cinnamon; knead thoroughly to mix. Roll out to ⅛" thickness on waxed paper dusted with confectioners sugar.

To another third of candy, add green food color mixed with 1 tsp. warm water and oil of peppermint. Knead to mix; roll out.

To final third of candy, add yellow food color mixed with 1 tsp. warm water and oil of lemon. Knead to mix; roll out.

Cut with very small cutters—hors d'oeuvre cutters with fancy shapes, if available, or use the inside of a doughnut cutter. Let the mints stand, bottom side up, on waxed paper at least 2 hours before placing in airtight con-tainers. Makes about 130 mints, or 1¼ pounds.

Christmas Ribbons

Three-layer candy looks like striped ribbon when sliced for servings

4½ c. sifted confectioners sugar
¼   c. melted butter or margarine
Few grains salt
1   tsp. vanilla
2   tblsp. (about) dairy half-and-half
1   square unsweetened chocolate, melted
⅓   c. chopped nuts
Green food color
2   tblsp. chopped, drained maraschino cherries

Combine 4¼ c. confectioners sugar, but-ter, salt and vanilla. Add enough half-and-half to make a mixture that holds its shape. Knead until smooth. Divide in thirds.

To one third add melted chocolate. To an-other third add nuts and a few drops of green food color to tint a delicate green. To the last third add chopped cherries and the remain-ing ¼ c. confectioners sugar. Mix each por-tion well.

Line an 11x4" ice cube tray with alumi-num foil. Spread and pat chocolate candy evenly in bottom of tray. Place the green candy on top, spreading and patting to make an even cover over chocolate layer. Then evenly spread candy with cherries on top. Place in refrigerator at least 1 hour. Remove from tray and slice. Makes about 1¼ pounds.

NOTE: If you do not plan to use candy at once, wrap the loaf in foil and store it in freezer or refrigerator. It will stay fresh and delicious for many weeks.

Chocolate Nut Roll

Hungry for candy but don't want to cook?
Here's your recipe

1 square unsweetened chocolate
1 egg white
⅛ tsp. salt
1½ to 2 c. sifted confectioners sugar
1 tblsp. soft butter
½ tsp. vanilla or rum extract
½ c. finely chopped pecans or walnuts
½ c. coarsely chopped pecans or walnuts

Melt chocolate in 1-qt. mixing bowl over hot water. Cool slightly.

In another bowl beat egg white with salt until stiff but not dry. Gradually add 1 c. confectioners sugar together with butter and vanilla. When well mixed, add to slightly cooled chocolate and blend.

Add remaining sugar, ¼ c. at a time, enough to make a stiff mixture. Mix sugar in thoroughly. Add finely chopped nuts just before the last addition of sugar, working them through the mixture.

Cut 2 (12x6") strips aluminum foil; place half of coarsely chopped nuts in center of each.

Form chocolate mixture into a ball; sprinkle lightly with confectioners sugar to prevent sticking to hands. Divide in half; form each half into a 6" roll. Place each roll on nuts and continue rolling, distributing nuts to cover entire roll, until it is 1" in diameter and 9" long. Roll up in the foil and place in refrigerator or freezer. Let stand several hours before using. Keeps indefinitely in freezer. Cut in ½ to ¾" slices to serve. Makes 24 (¾") or 36 (½") pieces, or ¾ pound.

Decorated Sugar Cubes

So pretty for a tea table

1 c. sifted confectioners sugar
3 tsp. hot water
Food colors
Sugar cubes

Mix confectioners sugar and water; add 1 to 2 drops food color to tint frosting in color desired (red for roses, blue for forget-me-nots, green for leaves—or as you prefer). Mixture should be stiff, colors should be dainty pastels.

With cake decorating tubes, make tiny flower and leaf design on sugar cubes (see photo in this book).

CONFECTIONS

Fruit Confections

Fruit Confections

Fruit confections are not new, but our recipes for them are—or they are revised versions of revered old timers. Dried apricot and apple confections, set with gelatin, rate as great regional favorites on the West Coast. Visitors to the area often ship or carry boxes of them home for gifts to family and friends. But you don't have to live in the far Western states to get these confections. You can make them with the recipes in this section, and many other fruit specials, too! Do try them soon.

Northwestern Apricot Candy

If you like apricots you'll enjoy this famous Northwestern treat

2   (5½ oz.) pkgs. dried apricots (2 c.)
1   c. warm water
2   c. sugar
1   tblsp. cornstarch
⅛   tsp. salt
2   tblsp. unflavored gelatin
½   c. cold water
½   to ⅔ c. chopped or slivered almonds,
       or chopped walnuts
⅓   c. confectioners sugar (for rolling)

Remove any stems or blemishes from apricots. Soak in warm water 1 hour, then cook slowly in same water until very tender, stirring to avoid scorching. Put through a food mill or sieve. Cook apricot pulp until thick in a 2-qt. heavy saucepan, stirring frequently to avoid scorching.

Mix sugar, cornstarch and salt and add to apricot pulp. Cook until very thick, stirring constantly.

Add gelatin, which has been softened in cold water. Stir until gelatin is dissolved and cook until mixture is again thick. Remove from heat.

Mix in almonds. Turn into a 9x7" shallow glass dish that has been rinsed with cold water. Let stand 24 hours.

Cut candy in rectangular pieces (about 60) and roll in confectioners sugar. Let stand on rack until outside has dried (texture should be slightly chewy). Store in covered container. Makes about 1 pound, 12 ounces, depending on amount of nuts used.

Northwestern Apple Candy

Be sure to dry these confections before storing

4 to 5 unpeeled apples
2 tblsp. unflavored gelatin
½ c. cold water
2 c. sugar
1 tblsp. cornstarch
⅛ tsp. salt
⅔ c. coarsely chopped walnuts
1 tsp. grated lemon peel
1 tblsp. lemon juice
⅓ c. confectioners sugar (for rolling)

Wash apples; without peeling or coring, cut in small pieces. Cook until very tender in just enough water to avoid scorching. Put through food mill or sieve and measure 2 c. pulp into a 2-qt. heavy saucepan. Cook until thick, stirring often.

Soften gelatin in cold water.

Mix sugar, cornstarch and salt; add to apple pulp. Cook again over low heat, stirring constantly, until mixture is very thick. Add gelatin; stir until gelatin is dissolved and mixture is again thick. Remove from heat.

Stir in walnuts, lemon peel and juice. Turn into an 8″ square shallow glass dish that has been rinsed with cold water. Let stand 24 hours.

Cut rectangles (about 60). Roll in confectioners sugar, and place on rack until outside is dry. Store in covered container. Makes about 1 pound, 12 ounces.

NOTE: You can use 2 c. sweetened canned applesauce to make this confection, but reduce the amount of sugar from 2 to 1⅓ cups.

Apricot-Orange Balls

With the demand for dried apricots so great, the price tag on them is higher, but they are worth the cost, especially for gala occasions

1 large orange
3 (5½ oz.) pkgs. dried apricots
2 c. sugar
⅔ c. (about) sugar (for rolling)

Peel orange; remove white lining from peel and membrane from sections; remove any seeds.

Put apricots, orange sections and peel through food chopper using fine or medium blade (alternate ingredients to make grinding easier). Turn into a 3-qt. heavy saucepan; add 2 c. sugar and cook over medium heat about 8 minutes, stirring continuously. At this stage the mixture will drop from spoon in large pieces.

Remove from heat at once and allow to cool 30 minutes, or until a spoonful dropped in sugar can be handled easily and rolled into a ball.

Place ⅔ c. sugar in a small bowl or cup. Using 2 teaspoons, dip a small amount of apricot mixture in sugar with one, pushing it out with the second spoon. Form quickly into a ball. Repeat with remaining apricot mixture. Place on sugar-sprinkled waxed paper to cool and set. Let stand several hours before packing in airtight containers. Makes 7 to 8 dozen balls the diameter of a 50-cent piece, or about 2 pounds.

Apricot Nuggets

These easy-to-make candies add a tasty note to a plate of confections

1 lb. confectioners sugar
6 tblsp. melted butter or margarine
2 tblsp. orange juice
½ tsp. vanilla
1 (11 oz.) pkg. dried apricots, ground (about 1½ c.)
1 c. chopped pecans

Combine sugar, butter, orange juice and vanilla. Add apricots. Mix, then knead in bowl until ingredients are well mixed.

Form into 1″ balls. Roll in chopped nuts. Store in refrigerator or freezer in covered container. Flavor improves with storage. Makes 6 dozen candies.

NOTE: If you like, you can omit the pecans and roll the candy balls in 1½ c. shredded coconut.

Buttered Stuffed Dates

You'll be surprised how heating dates in butter steps up flavor

1 (12 oz.) pkg. pitted dates
2 tblsp. butter
⅓ c. (about) salted cashew or mixed salted nuts
⅓ c. (about) sifted confectioners sugar

Remove any stem ends from dates; set aside.

Melt butter in 8″ heavy skillet over medium heat. Add dates, one at a time, and cook 6 to 8 minutes, stirring with a rubber spatula. Remove from heat and let stand in skillet to cool until easy to handle.

Meanwhile, sort out 42 perfect cashews, peanuts or almonds. Stuff each date with 1 nut (you may need more for large dates).

Drop stuffed dates, about 6 at a time, into confectioners sugar; shake off any excess sugar. Continue until all dates are coated. Wrap individually in waxed paper twisting ends. Makes about 42 pieces, depending on number of dates in package, or 1 pound.

NOTE: You may also stuff dates with small or halved Brazil nuts, but be sure to heat them first with butter and a little salt.

Walnut-Stuffed Prunes

Sugar coating melts during the time the stuffed fruit mellows

1 lb. dried prunes
1 c. walnut pieces
18 marshmallows, cut in pieces
¼ c. sugar

Slit sides of soft dried prunes and carefully remove pits. Stuff with walnut and marshmallow pieces. Roll in sugar.

Place in waxed paper-lined coffee cans or other containers. Cover tightly and store in a cool place several days or weeks. Makes about 48, depending on size of prunes.

NOTE: To cut up marshmallows easily, dip scissors in cold water.

Popcorn Confections

Honeyed Popcorn

Honey makes these different. Serve to children who come to visit

```
 3   qts. popped corn
1½  c. sugar
 ½  c. honey
 1   tsp. salt
 2   tblsp. butter or margarine
 1   tsp. vanilla
```

Turn popped corn into bowl.

Combine sugar, honey and salt in small saucepan. Heat and stir to dissolve sugar. Boil to hard ball stage (260°). Add butter and vanilla. Pour syrup over popped corn, stirring gently to coat kernels.

Drop by tablespoons onto waxed paper. When popcorn is cool enough to handle, butter hands and quickly shape into bite-size balls. Store in airtight container at room temperature. Makes 24 balls.

Oven-Made Caramel Corn

Be ready for evening callers—make this inexpensive snack the new, easy way. A fine gift to mail to youngsters away at school

```
 5   qts. popped corn
 1   c. butter or margarine (2 sticks)
 2   c. brown sugar, firmly packed
 ½  c. light corn syrup
 1   tsp. salt
 ½  tsp. baking soda
```

Spread freshly popped corn in a large, shallow sheet pan. Put it in a very slow oven (250°) to keep warm and crisp.

Combine butter, brown sugar, corn syrup and salt in 2-qt. heavy saucepan. Place on medium heat, stirring until sugar dissolves. Continue to boil to the firm ball stage (248°), about 5 minutes.

Remove from heat and stir in baking soda. Syrup will foam.

Take popped corn from oven and pour hot caramel mixture over it in a fine stream. Stir to mix well. Return to oven for 45 to 50 minutes, stirring every 15 minutes. Cool and serve, or store.

To store, pour into airtight containers and set in a cold place. Makes about 5 quarts, or almost 2 pounds.

Popcorn Nibble-Ons

This makes a fine candy go-with—complements the sweet taste

3 qts. popped corn
2 c. cheese snack crackers or nibblers
2 c. salted Spanish peanuts
2 c. pretzel sticks
⅓ c. melted butter
½ tsp. bottled steak sauce
½ tsp. garlic salt
½ tsp. onion salt
½ tsp. curry powder
½ tsp. salt

Combine popped corn, crackers, peanuts and pretzel sticks in large roasting pan.

Combine remaining ingredients and add to first mixture. Toss to mix.

Heat in very slow oven (250°) about 1 hour, stirring every 15 minutes. Cool. Store in airtight container. Makes about 4½ quarts.

NOTE: These Popcorn Nibble-Ons can be made ahead, packed in airtight containers and stored in the freezer. They will keep for several months, and are good to have on hand to serve guests.

Popcorn-on-Sticks

Perfect for party favors. Children and adults like to munch on them

1½ c. sugar
¾ c. light corn syrup
½ c. water
¼ tsp. salt
3 tblsp. butter
2½ qts. popped corn

Combine sugar, corn syrup, water and salt in 2-qt. heavy saucepan. Place over low heat, stirring until mixture boils. Cook without stirring to the soft crack stage (270°).

Remove from heat; add butter, stirring only enough to combine with syrup.

Pour syrup over popped corn in a large greased bowl, using a wooden spoon to mix until every kernel is coated. For attractive results, divide syrup in 3 parts; delicately tint each with a few drops of food color, such as green, red and yellow.

With lightly greased hands, form popcorn cylinders to put on sticks; don't press too hard. Or press the syrup-coated corn into small greased juice cans; remove can bottoms to push out cylinders.

Cereal Confections

Cereal Confections

Cereal snacks actually challenge candy in popularity because they so successfully appease the craving for sweets. Another plus: These confections are simple to fix and are relatively inexpensive.

Be sure to try some of our recipes. You'll really brighten a box of Christmas cookies or a plate of candy if you include some Tiny Holiday Wreaths fashioned with corn flakes. Our taste panel voted them among the ten most beautiful and tasty treats made with recipes in this cookbook. The chances are good that you'll agree with this rating.

Tiny Holiday Wreaths

Candied corn flakes look like holly—you even add red "berries"

30 marshmallows
½ c. butter (1 stick)
1 tsp. vanilla
2 tsp. green food color
3½ c. corn flakes
Small red candies (for decorating)

Combine marshmallows, butter, vanilla and food color (2 tsp. is correct) in top of double boiler. Heat over water until marshmallows and butter are melted, stirring frequently.

Gradually stir in corn flakes.

Drop from teaspoon onto waxed paper; with hands shape into tiny wreaths, about 1½ to 2″ in diameter. Decorate with small red candies (tiny red hots or other small candies). Makes 33 (2″) wreaths.

NOTE: Instead of tiny wreaths, you can make one big Holiday Wreath. Drop mixture from spoon in a circle onto waxed paper; with hands, shape to make a 9″ wreath. Decorate with red candied cherries and silver dragees.

Butterscotch Haystacks

Crisp and sweet and so easy to make

2 (6 oz.) pkgs. butterscotch-flavored
    morsels
1½ c. salted cashew nuts
1 (5 oz.) can chow mein noodles

Melt butterscotch bits in top of double boiler, stirring occasionally to blend.

Meanwhile, combine nuts and chow mein noodles; place in preheated low oven (200°). Add warmed nuts and noodles to melted butterscotch and stir until all are coated.

Quickly drop with a dessert spoon onto waxed paper-lined baking sheet to form little haystacks. If nuts and noodles are warmed, butterscotch will not set until all the stacks are spooned out. Makes 48 haystacks, or about 1 pound.

NOTE: You can substitute 1½ c. salted peanuts for the cashews, if you wish.

Butterscotch Cereal Toss

Snack is crunchy—butterscotch coating provides rich flavor

2 qts. assorted bite-size, ready-to-serve
    cereals
1 c. salted peanuts
2 c. pretzel sticks
½ c. butter
1½ c. brown sugar
¼ c. dark corn syrup
½ tsp. salt
¼ tsp. ground nutmeg
1 tsp. vanilla

Combine cereals, peanuts and pretzel sticks in large pan or bowl.

Combine butter, brown sugar, corn syrup, salt and nutmeg in saucepan. Bring to a boil; boil 2 minutes. Remove from heat; add vanilla. Pour over cereal mixture; stir to coat all ingredients.

Spread on 2 buttered baking sheets. Let cool until firm. To hasten cooling, place in refrigerator. When set, break in pieces. Makes about 3 quarts.

Bread, Crackers and Cookies

Bread, Cracker and Cookie

When you want to fix confections that please, reach into the breadbox, or open a box of store cookies, graham or soda crackers. With these modest foods you can create some of today's best confections. The recipes in this section show you how to do it.

These confections have many charms. They make exceptionally good eating. They are fast to fix. And they are kind to the pocketbook. That's about all you have a right to expect of any snacks.

Holiday Meringue Squares

Almonds and cherries make this a holiday special

¼	c. butter
1	c. blanched almonds (or other nuts)
2	egg whites
¼	tsp. cream of tartar
½	tsp. salt
1	tsp. vanilla
1	c. sugar
½	c. crushed soda crackers
1	(6 oz.) pkg. chocolate chips or milk chocolate chips (1 c.)
1	c. halved candied cherries

Heat butter and almonds in small saucepan; cool to room temperature.

Beat egg whites, cream of tartar, salt and vanilla until foamy. Gradually add sugar, beating until the mixture is stiff.

Fold in crackers, chocolate chips and cherries. (Wipe cherries with paper toweling to remove traces of syrup.) Carefully fold in nuts. Spread in a well-buttered 13x9x2" pan.

Bake in moderate oven (350°) 30 to 35 minutes, or until golden brown. While warm, cut into bars or squares of desired size. Makes 24 (about 2") squares.

VARIATION

Cherry/Nut Meringues: Omit chocolate pieces from Holiday Meringue Squares; bake and cut in the same way.

Nut Meringue Squares

Take your pick of baked meringue cut in squares or broken in pieces

2½ c. mixed salted nuts (13 oz.)
¼ c. melted butter
2 egg whites
¼ tsp. cream of tartar
¼ tsp. salt
1 tsp. vanilla
1 c. sugar
½ c. crushed soda crackers

Combine nuts and butter.

Beat egg whites, cream of tartar, salt and vanilla until foamy. Add sugar gradually, continuing to beat until meringue is stiff.

Fold in crushed crackers (crumbs) and then carefully fold in nuts. Spread into well-buttered 13x9x2″ pan.

Bake in moderate oven (350°) 30 to 35 minutes, or until golden brown. Cut in squares (about 2″) while warm. Cool. Makes 24 squares.

VARIATION

Nut Meringue Flakes: Let Nut Meringue cool without cutting in squares. Then break in pieces.

Frozen Chocolate Cups

This frozen chocolate confection is finger food. It makes a delightful small dessert to serve at a buffet supper

1 c. butter (2 sticks)
2 c. confectioners sugar
4 squares unsweetened chocolate, melted
4 eggs, beaten
1 tsp. rum or peppermint extract
1 tsp. vanilla
1½ c. vanilla wafer crumbs
36 small paper baking cups about 1¼″ across bottom)

Place butter in large bowl of electric mixer and allow to stand at room temperature until soft. Add confectioners sugar, and cream together by hand. Add chocolate, eggs and flavorings; beat with electric mixer until thoroughly combined and fluffy, 2 to 3 minutes.

Place 1 tsp. vanilla wafer crumbs in bottom of each paper cup. Set each in a paper nut cup of similar size to reinforce cup that holds confection. Or set in smallest size muffin-pan cups, if you have them.

With a pointed teaspoon (not rounded measuring spoon), fill two thirds full of chocolate mixture, rounding top slightly. Sprinkle top of each with additional 1 tsp. crumbs.

Place on trays and put in freezer. When frozen solid, remove candy cups from supporting nut cups or muffin-pan cups. Package them in a box with waxed paper between layers, wrap in aluminum foil and put in freezer. Or put in plastic bags; close tightly and freeze (they keep indefinitely in freezer).

When ready to use, remove from freezer and serve in the cups. Makes 36 confections.

Orange/Chocolate Balls

Taste-testers really liked these

3	c. vanilla wafer crumbs (12 oz. pkg.)
1	c. sifted confectioners sugar
¼	c. cocoa
1½	c. finely chopped or ground walnuts
¼	c. light or dark corn syrup
½	c. frozen orange juice concentrate

Combine all ingredients in a 2-qt. mixing bowl. Mix and knead with hands to form solid masses, adding a little more corn syrup if necessary to make ingredients stick together.

Roll mixture into balls ¾ to 1″ in size. Store in airtight container in refrigerator and let stand a few days before serving; flavor improves on ripening. Makes 50 to 60 pieces, or 2 pounds.

NOTE: You can give the balls a frosted look by rolling them in confectioners sugar.

Chocolate-Coated Crispies

You dip toasted bread in chocolate and come up with a great treat!

6	slices bread
1	tblsp. melted butter
1	(6 oz.) pkg. chocolate chips
2	tblsp. shortening

Trim crusts from bread. Butter slices lightly. Cut in 1″ squares. Toast in very slow oven (250°) 1 hour, turning every 15 minutes.

Melt chocolate chips with shortening in saucepan over low heat. Stir until smooth. Remove from heat.

With 2 forks, dip squares of bread in chocolate to coat. Place on wire rack to permit chocolate to set. Makes about 8 dozen squares.

VARIATION

Chocolate-Coated Crackerettes: Spread 2 c. oyster crackers in shallow pan. Brush lightly with butter. Toast and dip in chocolate like bread squares.

Mystery Drops

Crackers are mystery ingredient. Candy is easy to make, really good

2	c. sugar
⅔	c. milk
¾	c. finely ground soda cracker crumbs (30 crackers)
½	c. finely chopped pecans
1	tsp. vanilla
7	tblsp. smooth or crunchy peanut butter

Combine sugar and milk in 2-qt. heavy saucepan. Bring to a boil, stirring until sugar is dissolved. Boil 3 minutes. Remove from heat.

Add remaining ingredients, mixing quickly. Beat until mixture is thick enough to drop from teaspoon onto waxed paper. Makes 33 drops or about 1½ pounds.

Skillet Caramel Crispies

Confection starts out as bread . . . serve it with fruit juice or tea

½   c. brown sugar
½   c. butter
¼   c. finely chopped nuts (optional)
24 (2″) bread squares (day old bread)

Melt brown sugar and butter together in small saucepan. Boil 2 minutes. Add nuts. Remove from heat.

Dip bread squares in hot brown sugar mixture and fry in buttered skillet over medium heat until golden and caramel-like on both sides. Turn every 2 or 3 minutes while browning. Total time for pan-frying is 8 to 10 minutes. (You can dip more squares in caramel that melts off into skillet during cooking.) Cool on racks. Makes 24.

VARIATION

Coconut Caramel Crispies: Substitute ¼ c. flaked coconut for the nuts.

Napoleon Cremes

Creamy layered confections to cut in little pieces—they're rich!

½   c. butter (1 stick)
¼   c. sugar
¼   c. cocoa
1   tsp. vanilla
1   egg, slightly beaten
2   c. graham cracker crumbs
1   c. flake coconut
½   c. butter (1 stick)
3   tblsp. milk
1   (3¾ oz.) vanilla instant pudding mix
2   c. sifted confectioners sugar
1   (6 oz.) pkg. chocolate chips
2   tblsp. butter
1   tblsp. paraffin (optional)

Combine ½ c. butter, sugar, cocoa and vanilla in top of double boiler. Cook over simmering water until butter melts. Stir in egg. Continue cooking, stirring, until mixture is thick, about 3 minutes. Blend in crumbs and coconut. Press into buttered 9″ square pan.

Cream ½ c. butter thoroughly. Stir in milk, pudding mix and confectioners sugar. Beat until light and fluffy. Spread evenly over crust. Chill until firm.

Melt chocolate, 2 tblsp. butter and paraffin over simmering water. Cool. Spread over pudding layer. Chill. Cut in 2x¾″ bars. Makes about 44 pieces.

Turtle Shells

Children love to mold turtles from crumb-coated chocolate mixture

1½ c. sugar
1 (6 oz.) can evaporated milk (⅔ c.)
2 squares unsweetened chocolate
1 (6¼ oz.) pkg. miniature marshmallows
½ c. chopped pecans
1 c. graham cracker crumbs
1 tsp. vanilla

Combine sugar, evaporated milk and chocolate in 1-qt. heavy saucepan. Bring to a full rolling boil, stirring constantly until sugar dissolves and chocolate blends into mixture. Set aside to cool.

Combine marshmallows and nuts in a big bowl; mix well.

Put cracker crumbs in a shallow pan.

When chocolate mixture is cool, but not cold, add vanilla. Pour over marshmallows and nuts and stir carefully. Drop by spoonfuls onto cracker crumbs. Roll each spoonful of candy to coat with crumbs, then shape like a turtle shell. Place on waxed paper to set, 30 minutes of longer. Makes about 1½ pounds.

Mock Almond Crunch

Baked confection made with graham crackers —tastes like toffee

9 graham crackers
⅓ c. sliced almonds
½ c. brown sugar
½ c. butter
⅛ tsp. almond extract
⅓ c. milk chocolate chips or
      chocolate chips

Arrange graham cracker squares on bottom of buttered 9″ square pan. Sprinkle with almond slices.

Combine brown sugar and butter in small saucepan. Boil 3 minutes. Remove from heat and add almond extract. Pour over graham crackers.

Bake in slow oven (325°) 10 minutes. Remove from oven.

When mixture stops bubbling, sprinkle with chocolate chips. Let stand 10 minutes. Then spread chocolate to frost. Cut in 1½″ squares while warm. Makes 36.

Index